I0605924
TO:
FROM:
DATE:

— A GUIDED JOURNAL —

Praying the Word

— 90 —

SCRIPTURE-POWERED PRAYERS to Calm an Anxious Heart

LINDA EVANS SHEPHERD

Christian Art
PUBLISHERS

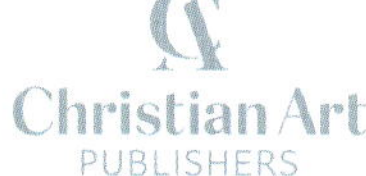

Visit Christian Art Gifts, Inc., at www.christianartgifts.com.

Praying the Word: 90 Scripture-Powered Prayers to Calm an Anxious Heart

Published by Christian Art Gifts, Inc., Bloomingdale, IL, USA.

Published in association with the Books & Such Literary Management, www.booksandsuch.com.

First edition 2025.

Designed by Christian Art Gifts, Inc.

Cover and interior images used under license from Shutterstock.com.

Most Christian Art titles may be purchased at bulk discounts by churches, nonprofits, and corporations. For more information, please email SpecialMarkets@cagifts.com.

ISBN 979-8-89678-191-2

Printed in China.

30 29 28 27 26 25
10 9 8 7 6 5 4 3 2 1

To the amazing women
I am blessed to do life with—
your faith and friendship
inspire me as we serve Jesus together.
Through His love, we strengthen
each other, shine His light,
and make an eternal impact.
Thank you for walking this
journey of purpose
and ministry by my side.

Table of Contents

INTRODUCTION

And the peace of God, which surpasses all understanding, will guard your hearts and your minds in Christ Jesus.

Philippians 4:7 ESV

Has a particular worry ever troubled you, one that never came true? If so, I have good news: most of the things we imagine never happen.

When I was five, I loved the story of the Three Little Pigs—except for the Big Bad Wolf. I was convinced he was hiding behind my curtains, and every night, I stayed awake, terrified that my imaginary wolf was lurking in the dark.

Maybe you can relate. Perhaps, like me, you're wrestling with worries that either aren't real or will never happen. But maybe you're dealing with the painful bite of real trouble.

To combat my fears and heartaches, I developed a strategy for peace. Finding peace is what kept me going during a terrible family tragedy. No doubt about it, God's peace transformed my broken heart.

A few years after learning how to experience peace in the midst of life's storms, I was invited to teach a class on peace at a workshop in Denver. Our small classroom was packed, barely able to contain the hurting women who came to listen. As I spoke, God's peace filled the room. I was amazed at how deeply my message resonated with the audience. Since then, I've shared this message of peace with hundreds of thousands of people.

What about you? Do you need more peace? Let's begin our journey together by reading one of God's promises for peace: "The LORD gives strength to his people; the LORD blesses his people with peace" (Psalm 29:11 NIV).

Let's pray based on this promise:

Dear Lord,

I know what it's like to live in weakness, but You promise to give me strength. I believe Your strength is for me, and I say, "Thank You!"

You also promise me peace, and I receive it with joy. Your peace is my secret weapon against anxiety and fear.

The enemy of my soul wants me to tremble at my own imaginations, but I refuse to fall for his tactics. Instead, Lord, I kneel before You and ask that You remove any false imaginations from my mind.

When it comes to my troubles, I give each one to You, Lord.

You are not only the God who gives me peace, but You are also the God who turns my troubles into blessings. Why should I be afraid?

Thank You, Lord, for taking me on a fresh journey to peace through both prayer and Your Word.

In the name of Jesus, Amen.

I am so glad that you're joining me on this journey toward peace.

You can use this book in whatever way works best for you. You can read it from beginning to end, as you would a devotional, or you can use the contents page to find prayers that meet your current needs. As you pray through this book, you'll notice that each prayer closely reflects the Scripture passages that accompany it. This is intentional because God loves it when we pray His Word back to Him.

His Word is alive and powerful—it can bring us peace. Praying Scripture gives us the confidence that we're not only praying according to His will, but we're also agreeing with and embracing His promises for us. Be sure to spend time meditating on the Scripture passages connected to each prayer, as God's Word is a source of transformative power.

When you find a Scripture passage that speaks to you, take time to meditate on it by rereading it. Then, use it to craft your own prayer. This is a way to continue praying while experiencing God's peaceful presence.

Pray your personalized prayer often. Consider memorizing the Scripture passages so that you can recall them whenever you need them.

You may notice that some Scripture verses appear more than once throughout the prayers. This is intentional. God's Word is living and active, and certain promises carry deep, layered meaning that applies to more than one topic or situation. By revisiting key verses in different prayer contexts, you'll discover new insights and fresh encouragement. Just as a favorite worship song can minister to us in many seasons, God's promises have the power to meet us right where we are, again and again. Likewise, each devotional has one verse marked in bold; these are verses you may find especially helpful to meditate on or even memorize.

And don't hesitate to read prayers that you may not relate to right now. The time may come when you'll need the peace those prayers offer. Also, explore the inspirational prayers that can help you overcome your fears.

God bless you as you journey toward the bliss of peace.

–1–

Abiding in the Vine

MEDITATE ON THE WORD

Abide in me, and I in you.
As the branch cannot bear fruit by itself,
unless it abides in the vine,
neither can you,
unless you abide in me.

JOHN 15:4 ESV

No one has ever seen God. But if we love each other,
God lives in us, and his love is brought to full expression in us.
And God has given us his Spirit as proof that we live in him and he in us.

1 JOHN 4:12-13 NLT

But the Holy Spirit produces this kind of fruit in our lives:
love, joy, peace, patience, kindness, goodness,
faithfulness, gentleness, and self-control.
There is no law against these things!

GALATIANS 5:22-23 NLT

I am the vine; you are the branches. If you remain in me and I in you,
you will bear much fruit; apart from me you can do nothing.

JOHN 15:5 NIV

---

*Therefore, if anyone is in Christ, he is a new creation.
The old has passed away; behold, the new has come.*

2 CORINTHIANS 5:17 ESV

CONTEMPLATE IN PRAYER

Dear Lord,

The roots of the grapevine burrow deep into the soil, and when the sun warms the earth, the vine sends out green shoots that unfurl tender tendrils to climb the garden gate. The trunk of the vine supports these mini branches with life, soon filling them with abundant leaves. These little branches continue to drink the sap from the vine's trunk, nourishing tiny clusters of blossoms. In due season, the blossoms' petals fall away, revealing tiny green bulbs that transform into bunches of grapes, plump with sweetness and delight.

But make no mistake—even though the fruit is connected to the branches, the branches are connected to the vine—the grapes receive their life from the vine.

This miracle would never happen if the branch snapped free from the vine, for the branch cannot produce fruit without the life that flows from the vine.

Lord, You reveal this as a picture of me. My soul cannot mature unless it's nourished by You—by Your love and the peace of Your ever-present Holy Spirit flowing into my life. If I am cut off from You, not only do I wither, but so does my fruit. But if I abide in You, Your sweetness transforms me into a brand-new person filled with Your love. Besides the fruit of love, Your Spirit produces the fruit of joy, peace, patience, kindness, goodness, faithfulness, gentleness, and self-control.

May I continue to abide in You as You continue to abide in me. My life carries the sweetness of Your purpose and bears much fruit when I remain connected to You.

In the name of Jesus, Amen.

REFLECT FROM YOUR HEART

1. Your life can be like a thick, healthy vine branch covered with grapes when it is attached to the vine of Christ. What spiritual fruit would you like to see produced in your life?

2. Weeds and brambles can choke the fruitfulness of a healthy vine. What weeds in your life rob you of spiritual fruitfulness? How can you intentionally uproot them and keep them from returning?

3. A healthy branch abides in the vine without striving to do so. What steps can you take to fully embrace this restful abiding with Christ and experience deeper spiritual growth?

–2–

Acceptance

MEDITATE ON THE WORD

And everyone who calls on the name of the Lord will be saved.

ACTS 2:21 NIV

Look! I stand at the door and knock. If you hear my voice and open the door, I will come in, and we will share a meal together as friends.

REVELATION 3:20 NLT

For there is no difference between Jew and Gentile—
the same Lord is Lord of all and richly blesses all who call on him,
for, "Everyone who calls on the name of the Lord will be saved."

ROMANS 10:12-13 NIV

Accept one another, then, just as Christ accepted you, in order to bring praise to God.

ROMANS 15:7 NIV

But to all who believed him and accepted him, he gave the right to become children of God.

JOHN 1:12 NLT

CONTEMPLATE IN PRAYER

Dear Lord,

I once lived in a gray world, absent of all color. All I could see was my shame and the darkness of my own sin. One day, while I wallowed in hopelessness, I caught a glimpse of light—a light filled with peace and living color. In that moment, I saw there was life beyond my void.

The light I found was the hope glowing from Your beautiful name, JESUS!

I was surprised when my blindness lifted to reveal You, so I called, "Jesus, please rescue me!" The light of Your love erased the shadows that held me prisoner. You not only set me free to experience Your peace, but You also adopted me and called me Yours simply because I believed in Your name.

And because I have opened the door of my life to You, You have come in to feed my starving soul. You sit down at the table of fellowship and talk with me over Your Word. You even call me Your friend.

I realized we are not alone, for others have joined us. You have intended for all who have called on Your name to be Your friend. No matter our race or station in life, we are all one with You.

You call us to accept one another in You, just as You have accepted all of us simply because we called upon Your name. So together we lift our voices and not only praise who You are, but we also thank You for who we are in You—Yours. We thank You for Your holy name.

Thank You for accepting me completely, just as I am, in grace.

In the name of Jesus, Amen.

REFLECT FROM YOUR HEART

1. Have you transitioned from living in a gray world to the peace of seeing the light of Jesus? If not, now is a good time to call upon the powerful name of Jesus to help you and guide you.

2. Take some time thanking Jesus for all the ways He has set you free and continues to do so.

3. When we call upon Jesus, we are united with other believers who have also called on His name. How does this realization help you embrace your place in the community of Christ, and what can you do to actively serve and contribute to the community?

–3–

Addiction

MEDITATE ON THE WORD

Jesus looked at them and said, "With man this is impossible,
but with God all things are possible."

MATTHEW 19:26 NIV

My God will richly fill your every need in a glorious way through Christ Jesus.

PHILIPPIANS 4:19 GW

For we do not have a high priest who is unable to empathize with our weaknesses, but we have one who has been tempted in every way, just as we are—yet he did not sin. Let us then approach God's throne of grace with confidence, so that we may receive mercy and find grace to help us in our time of need.

HEBREWS 4:15-16 NIV

And I will do whatever you ask in my name,
so that the Father may be glorified in the Son.

JOHN 14:13 NIV

If any of you lacks wisdom, you should ask God, who gives generously to all without finding fault, and it will be given to you.

JAMES 1:5 NIV

CONTEMPLATE IN PRAYER

Dear Lord,

I am bound by chains I cannot break, like a wild animal caught in a trap. I have tried everything humanly possible to set myself free, but my struggles have only tightened my bonds. Finding freedom is impossible in my own strength, but Your Word says freedom can be found in You.

I've failed to escape my chains by myself, I now realize I need Your help. For You have promised to give me wisdom without judging me for my lack of understanding. Please show me what I need to do to sever my restraints.

As I ask You to set me free from the traps of the enemy, I trust You will reveal the key to unlock my bonds so I can step into the glorious richness of Your freedom.

For You are my High Priest who understands my needs even when I am weak. You faced temptation just like me, but unlike me, You were sinless and rose above every trap.

I see You, Jesus, lifted high, sitting on Your throne. I am amazed You extend Your grace to me. I am confident I will find Your mercy, grace, and peace, as well as Your victory.

This is why I call upon Your name, knowing that if I ask You to set me free, You will do it! In awe, I call upon You now. I breathe in Your love, and in this moment, I am set free from my chains by the power of God through the name of Jesus.

Thank You, Lord, for Your constant presence, guiding me toward lasting freedom and healing.

In the name of Jesus, Amen.

REFLECT FROM YOUR HEART

1. Have you ever struggled with an addiction, whether to a substance, need for control, or approval from others, that needed divine intervention for you to break free? If you are currently facing such an addiction, call on the name of Jesus to help you now.

2. Jesus overcame every temptation, while we humans often stumble into sin. How does the sinlessness of Jesus impact your personal faith journey?

3. We have victory through Jesus, but to receive victory, we must want it and ask for it. Pray for God to set you free from whatever sin is holding you captive and know that Jesus' victory is sufficient to break any chains. Pray peace over your own life and the life of your friends and family.

–4–

Anger

MEDITATE ON THE WORD

Control your temper, for anger labels you a fool.
ECCLESIASTES 7:9 NLT

Whoever is patient has great understanding,
but one who is quick-tempered displays folly.
PROVERBS 14:29 NIV

"In your anger do not sin":
Do not let the sun go down while you are still angry.
EPHESIANS 4:26 NIV

But I tell you that anyone who is angry
with a brother or sister will be subject to judgment.
Again, anyone who says to a brother or sister,
"Raca," is answerable to the court. And anyone who says,
"You fool!" will be in danger of the fire of hell.
MATTHEW 5:22 NIV

---

*Know this, my beloved brothers: let every person be quick to hear,
slow to speak, slow to anger; for the anger of man
does not produce the righteousness of God.*
JAMES 1:19-20 ESV

CONTEMPLATE IN PRAYER

Dear Lord,

Sometimes, when my soul feels dry, a hot wind blows a tiny spark of unrighteous anger into my life, and I explode like an inferno, burning anyone in my way.

How foolish it is to be so combustible, for when my temper calms, I see crumbling charcoal where my best relationships once stood.

Help me to stay cool-headed and filled with Your patience so that I do not destroy the people You have placed in my life.

Help me not to lose control, even when I am angry over injustice. Give me the calm only You can give. Otherwise, folly may ensnare me whenever I fall into a blind rage. Show me how to let go of anger so that when I place my head on my pillow, anger will not wrestle away my sleep.

Help me to listen instead of reacting like a hothead. Teach me how to be silent when I'm ready to lose it. Make a way for me to cool down and follow You into righteousness.

For anger can not only destroy my love for You, anger can also cause me to say harmful words I can't take back. Anger can even put me in danger of Your judgment.

So, here and now, I ask You to replace my anger with Your presence, kindness, and love as I invite Your Holy Spirit to replace any spirit of rage within me. Give me the wisdom to call on the name of Jesus instead of using His name in vain. Calm my heart and forgive me for my wounding words or careless reactions as You show me how to dwell in Your peace.

In the name of Jesus, Amen.

REFLECT FROM YOUR HEART

1. Can you recall a time when anger caused lasting damage in your life or someone else's? How was it resolved? If it hasn't been resolved, ask God for His peace and resolution.

2. How can one actively replace anger with God's presence, kindness, and love?

3. Ask the Lord to replace the spirit of rage in you, over you, or around you with the peace of the Holy Spirit. What practical steps can you take to invite the Holy Spirit into your life when you feel anger rising?

–5–

Anxiety

MEDITATE ON THE WORD

A person's anxiety will weigh him down,
but an encouraging word makes him joyful.

PROVERBS 12:25 GW

Turn all your anxiety over to God because he cares for you.

1 PETER 5:7 GW

I will instruct you and teach you in the way you should go;
I will counsel you with my eye upon you. Be not like a horse or a mule,
without understanding, which must be curbed with bit and bridle,
or it will not stay near you. Many are the sorrows of the wicked,
but steadfast love surrounds the one who trusts in the LORD.

PSALM 32:8-10 ESV

God didn't give us a cowardly spirit
but a spirit of power, love, and good judgment.

2 TIMOTHY 1:7 GW

Have I not commanded you? Be strong and courageous.
Do not be frightened, and do not be dismayed,
for the LORD your God is with you wherever you go.

JOSHUA 1:9 ESV

CONTEMPLATE IN PRAYER

Dear Lord,

Just when I think I'm in a good place, I start to worry. And worry releases the brakes on my roller-coaster life, plunging me into a downward spiral. The next thing I know, fear jerks me one way and then another.

I've learned I can put on the brakes by remembering 1 Peter 5:7, which says, "Turn all your anxiety over to God because he cares for you" (GW).

Okay, God, because You care, I give You my anxiety once again.

My wild ride slows, and I relax, glad to be in a calm place—that is until I start to worry again. But before I teeter into my downward spiral, I remember that You called me to be strong and not to lose faith. When I see You sitting right beside me, peace fills my heart, and the brakes on my anxiety hold fast.

I don't have to live on a roller coaster of worry. Your Word instructs me on how to get through my troubles with peace. Otherwise, I'm like a mule who needs a bridle because I wander off, trying to figure out solutions to my troubles by myself. This is when I give way to my fears, and I find myself spiraling into anxiety again. That happens whenever I forget that I can trust You and Your love for me.

You do not give me a cowardly spirit but a spirit of power, love, and good judgment. My thoughts calm whenever I remember that my life's companion is You—the God who loves me, guides me, and gives me peace.

Thank You, Lord, for calming my worries and restoring my peace always.

In the name of Jesus, Amen.

REFLECT FROM YOUR HEART

1. How can you apply the lessons from this prayer to live a life that is less controlled by the ups and downs of worry and more anchored in God's unshakable peace and trust? What are some practical steps you can take?

2. Take a moment to turn all your anxiety over to God. Create a heartfelt prayer of thanksgiving, expressing gratitude for His faithfulness.

3. Reflecting on the idea that peace fills your heart when recognizing God's presence, how do you practice acknowledging and feeling this divine companionship daily, especially during moments of stress or uncertainty?

–6–

Ashamed

MEDITATE ON THE WORD

For I am not ashamed of this Good News about Christ.
It is the power of God at work, saving everyone
who believes—the Jew first and also the Gentile.

ROMANS 1:16 NLT

Those who look to him are radiant;
their faces are never covered with shame.

PSALM 34:5 NIV

As the Scriptures tell us,
"Anyone who trusts in him will never be disgraced."

ROMANS 10:11 NLT

Instead of your shame you will receive a double portion,
and instead of disgrace you will rejoice in your inheritance.
And so you will inherit a double portion in your land,
and everlasting joy will be yours.

ISAIAH 61:7 NIV

He will neither fail you nor abandon you.

DEUTERONOMY 31:6 NLT

CONTEMPLATE IN PRAYER

Dear Lord,

When I look in the mirror, I see my warts, wrinkles, and frailties, and I feel ashamed of who I am. There is no way I will ever look like You. I will never be able to rise above my shame in my own strength.

But as I stare at my reflection, I realize I'm looking through the wrong eyes.

I turn to You, Jesus, and see You gazing into my soul. I see Your unconditional love as You lift Your nail-pierced hands toward me. You suffered for me, You took on my sin and human frailties, and You carried my shame to the cross. Then You rose above sin and death. When I look upon You, I am set free. Because You sacrificed Yourself on the cross for me, You paid the price for all my failures.

You astound me. You not only took my sin, but You also overcame my sin by rising from the grave—the holy, sinless One who is alive again! Not only did You do all of this for me, but You also made good on Your promise to never leave nor abandon me.

I will never be ashamed of You or this Good News because I am covered by the power of Your righteousness.

When I turn back to the mirror, I realize I reflect Your radiance because Your love has removed my sin. I will never be disgraced by who I used to be, for You give me more grace than I will ever deserve. You even give me a place in heaven so that I will be with You forever. I am filled with Your everlasting joy.

In the name of Jesus, Amen.

REFLECT FROM YOUR HEART

1. How does your perception of yourself change through Jesus' loving gaze? How can this new perspective of yourself transform your daily life and interactions with others?

2. Consider the imagery of Jesus lifting His nail-pierced hands toward you. How does the power of the cross impact your life and remind you of God's unconditional love and sacrifice?

3. Replace the mirrored image of your warts and wrinkles with an image of you reflecting Christ's radiance. How can you intentionally and daily reflect Christ's radiance to the people in your life, even in difficult situations?

–7–

Attitude

MEDITATE ON THE WORD

As holy people whom God has chosen and loved,
be sympathetic, kind, humble, gentle, and patient.
COLOSSIANS 3:12 GW

Therefore, accept each other in the same way that
Christ accepted you. He did this to bring glory to God.
ROMANS 15:7 GW

And let us consider how we may spur
one another on toward love and good deeds.
HEBREWS 10:24 NIV

Most important of all, continue to show deep love
for each other, for love covers a multitude of sins.
1 PETER 4:8 NLT

Be kind to each other, tenderhearted, forgiving one another,
just as God through Christ has forgiven you.
EPHESIANS 4:32 NLT

CONTEMPLATE IN PRAYER

Dear Lord,

There are days I find my spiritual and emotional "clothes" in the dirty-laundry basket, smeared with gripes and attitudes that stink.

But in my heart, I know this is not what You want me to wear. Because You love me and have chosen me to follow You, You have a different style for my life.

You convict me to cast aside my smelly garments, for You have given me a whole new closet filled with the freshness of compassion, kindness, humility, gentleness, and patience.

What surprises me most is that You want me to wear all these garments at once.

What I thought would be an uncomfortable fit makes me feel and look amazing. For when I wear the garments You designed, I can accept others in Your love, which is exactly the pattern You set when You accepted me in Your love.

When I dress up in this new look, I find I am kind and tenderhearted. It's suddenly easier to forgive others in the same way You've forgiven me.

When I top off my new look by wrapping myself in Your love, not only are my sins covered, but I also no longer judge the sins of those around me.

All of this makes me look good, do good, and be good, and I find myself representing Your patterns to others who need Your designer's touch.

I encourage others to try on this new look for themselves, so they too will do good, feel good, and love all those You have put into their lives.

Help me wear this attitude daily, reflecting Your love in all situations I face.

In the name of Jesus, Amen.

REFLECT FROM YOUR HEART

1. How does the idea of wearing compassion, kindness, humility, gentleness, and patience resonate with you? What makes these virtues essential garments for your spiritual journey, and how do they shape your interactions with others?

2. Are you wearing the smelly garments of negative attitudes? What practical steps can you take to recognize, shed, and replace these old rags with God's renewing love each day?

3. Wearing God's love prevents you from judging the sins of others. How can this new look transform conflicts into opportunities for growth, understanding, and lasting peace?

–8–

Balance

MEDITATE ON THE WORD

Whoever pursues righteousness and love finds life, prosperity and honor.

PROVERBS 21:21 NIV

First, help me never to tell a lie. Second, give me neither poverty nor riches! Give me just enough to satisfy my needs.

PROVERBS 30:8 NLT

But seek first his kingdom and his righteousness, and all these things will be given to you as well.

MATTHEW 6:33 NIV

For everything there is a season, and a time for every matter under heaven.

ECCLESIASTES 3:1 ESV

Do not be anxious about anything, but in every situation, by prayer and petition, with thanksgiving, present your requests to God.

PHILIPPIANS 4:6 NIV

CONTEMPLATE IN PRAYER

Dear Lord,

Following You is like traveling a path that leads me across streams and through valleys as I search for the gold of Your righteousness. This is the true treasure that brings not only contentment but also prosperity and honor. But when I chase after fool's gold instead of treasuring my life in You, neither poverty nor riches can satisfy my greedy heart.

Lord, this is why I thank You for providing my daily bread. Your provision is how You care for me and strengthen my body, mind, and spirit.

When I seek You, You give me all I need. You even grant me the strength to let go of my worldly desires so that I can escape the enemy's traps of fear and strife. I will remain in Your peace, no matter the trouble, need, or crisis I face.

You are with me in every season, no matter where I go or what I do. That's why I do not worry about the storms of life that catch me by surprise, for You are my shelter. I never need to be anxious about the troubles that tempt me to worry because I can always come to You in prayer, knowing that You are always listening. As I talk to You about my problems, I hand them over to You for safekeeping, trusting that You will work all things for good. You are my faithful companion, and I trust You to work out my problems without my help. Thank You for being so loving and faithful to me. I trust in You. You balance my life with Your peace.

In the name of Jesus, Amen.

REFLECT FROM YOUR HEART

1. What are some examples of fool's gold that we might pursue in our lives? How can we distinguish between false treasures and the true riches found in God's abundant love and grace?

2. Ask God to give you the strength to let go of worldly desires so you can escape fear and strife. How can surrendering your earthly ambitions lead to true peace and freedom in Christ's presence and power?

3. Why worry about life's storms when God is your shelter? Take a moment to seek God's peace amidst your storms and trust Him fully.

–9–

Be Still

MEDITATE ON THE WORD

The Lord is good to those who depend on him,
to those who search for him. So it is good
to wait quietly for salvation from the Lord.
Lamentations 3:25-26 NLT

There is a river whose streams make glad the city of God,
the holy place where the Most High dwells.
Psalm 46:4 NIV

The Lord is in his holy temple;
let all the earth be silent before him.
Habakkuk 2:20 NIV

He says, "Be still, and know that I am God;
I will be exalted among the nations, I will be exalted in the earth."
Psalm 46:10 NIV

The Lord will fight for you; you need only to be still.
Exodus 14:14 NIV

CONTEMPLATE IN PRAYER

Dear Lord,

I've been on a journey searching for Your presence. Then I realized You are always with me. All I needed to do was remind myself that You are here. So now I wait quietly in Your presence—not striving in prayer, not trying to convince You to act, but breathing and taking this moment to know that You are with me. I quietly worship You as I open my heart to Your love and drift into Your peace. As I rest in You, Your holiness pours out like a river from Your throne. Your solace flows throughout heaven in streams that gladden both the city and my heart.

Your presence dwells with your people, and all the earth is hushed before You. I, too, am silent, waiting on You, knowing You are with me.

You tell me, "Be still, and know that I am God."

I wait in quietness as my heart beats in Your presence, feeling Your love as You draw me close. Despite the chaos in this world, You *will* be exalted among the nations, and You *will* be exalted in the earth.

As I practice Your presence in this moment, there's no reason to plead or beg for favors or to spread my agenda before You. The only thing needed is stillness as I wait, knowing I can trust You, for You are the God who loves me, the God who fights for me.

I am Your child, delighted that You are near. As I wait on You, I wait in You. This encounter will strengthen me and fill me with Your peace as I go forth in Your love.

In the name of Jesus, Amen.

REFLECT FROM YOUR HEART

1. As we search for God, we come to a place where we realize He is always present. What practices and thoughts will help you stay aware that God is active in your daily life?

2. Breathe in and take this moment to recognize that God is with you. Describe what you feel as you remain in His presence.

3. Psalm 46:4 speaks of a river whose streams make glad the city of God. In what ways can you allow this peace to flow into different areas of your life?

–10–

Bitterness

MEDITATE ON THE WORD

Get rid of all bitterness, rage and anger,
brawling and slander, along with every form of malice.

Ephesians 4:31 niv

But if you harbor bitter envy and selfish ambition in your hearts,
do not boast about it or deny the truth.

James 3:14 niv

Bearing with one another and, if one has a complaint against another,
forgiving each other; as the Lord has forgiven you, so you also must forgive.

Colossians 3:13 esv

Make every effort to live in peace with everyone and to be holy;
without holiness no one will see the Lord. See to it that no one
falls short of the grace of God and that no bitter root
grows up to cause trouble and defile many.

Hebrews 12:14-15 niv

Keep your heart with all vigilance,
for from it flow the springs of life.

Proverbs 4:23 esv

CONTEMPLATE IN PRAYER

Dear Lord,

I would never think of drinking from a poisoned well, but neither should I allow poison to pollute my heart, for my heart is a spring of life. I must filter out toxins like bitterness to prevent unfiltered words or thoughts from seeping into my soul.

The sign that my heart has been poisoned is when I catch myself slandering others or spewing hatred. That's when I know I have a toxic spill that must be contained. If I harbor bitter envy, selfish ambition, boastfulness, or lies, then I know my soul has been polluted.

Teach me how to stop the flow of toxins like rage, anger, and hate that cause me to use my words like fists. If I am willing to fight to guard my wrong desires or brawl to protect my right to bitterness, I have blocked the flow of Your Spirit in my life.

To remove these poisons, I confess my sin and turn from it. When I do, new life springs into my heart, a life that flows from Your love. Help me to bear with the faults of others and teach me to forgive as You have forgiven me in Christ.

I will strive to live in peace with everyone as I learn to live a holy life. My heart will be renewed in You, Lord, and I can be assured that one day I will see You face-to-face.

Lord, help me not to fall short of Your grace. Help me uproot any bitter root poised to poison my heart or choke the life from my relationship with You.

In the name of Jesus, Amen.

REFLECT FROM YOUR HEART

1. It's important to keep our hearts from becoming a poisoned well. What are some common toxins that we allow into our hearts, and how can we actively filter them out daily?

2. The prayer speaks of God-flow bringing new life into our hearts. What practices or habits can help us cultivate this flow of love, kindness, and compassion regularly in our lives?

3. How does living in peace and striving for holiness, as mentioned in Hebrews 12, serve as safeguards against bitterness, resentment, and other spiritual toxins that hinder our growth?

–11–

Brokenness

MEDITATE ON THE WORD

The sacrifices of God are a broken spirit;
a broken and contrite heart, O God, you will not despise.

PSALM 51:17 ESV

My flesh and my heart may fail, but God is
the strength of my heart and my portion forever.

PSALM 73:26 NIV

The Spirit of the Sovereign LORD is upon me,
for the LORD has anointed me to bring good news to the poor.
He has sent me to comfort the brokenhearted and to proclaim
that captives will be released and prisoners will be freed.

ISAIAH 61:1 NLT

Heal me, O LORD, and I shall be healed; save me,
and I shall be saved, for you are my praise.

JEREMIAH 17:14 ESV

*The LORD is near to the brokenhearted
and saves the crushed in spirit.*

PSALM 34:18 ESV

CONTEMPLATE IN PRAYER

Dear Lord,

When my life shatters like glass, and I cannot pick up the pieces, You are there to put me back together. When I come to You broken and filled with regret, You restore my life. Even when my pain blinds me, and I cannot see You holding me together, You do not walk away but wait for me to see You. When I question Your love for me, You do not get offended because Your love remains. You gently carry me through this and every trial.

Because You paid for my restoration with the suffering of Your only Son, You heal my broken spirit. You allowed Jesus to be crushed by the weight of my sin. You endured incredible pain so that I could know Your love. The blood of Jesus brings me the gift of Your presence, even in this hour. Your presence allows me to rest in Your arms.

When I can no longer move forward in my own strength, You graciously give me Your strength. I am comforted knowing You are with me forever, holding me close for all eternity.

I have these gifts of restoration, forgiveness, healing, love, Your presence, and strength from You because You sent Your Son Jesus with the good news of Your salvation. Thank you that Jesus, the Resurrected One, sets me free from my sin, heals my broken heart, releases me from my prison of despair, and tends to my wounds.

As I learn to trust You through this pain, You give me Your peace and help me renew my life in You. I surrender my brokenness to You, knowing You heal me and I will be healed. My praise belongs to You.

In the name of Jesus, Amen.

REFLECT FROM YOUR HEART

1. How have you experienced God's presence in moments of suffering, even when you couldn't see Him clearly working? In what ways did His presence eventually become more evident to you?

2. Can you describe a time when you doubted God's love, feeling distant, but later realized He was faithfully carrying you through your troubles? How did this realization strengthen your relationship with Him and help you trust Him more?

3. What does it mean to you to rest in God's arms, especially in times of trial? How does this concept of resting align with the peace and healing mentioned in Isaiah 61:1? How do you practice resting in Him daily?

–12–

Calm

MEDITATE ON THE WORD

I am leaving you with a gift—peace of mind and heart.
And the peace I give is a gift the world cannot give.
So don't be troubled or afraid.

JOHN 14:27 NLT

This righteousness will bring peace.
Yes, it will bring quietness and confidence forever.

ISAIAH 32:17 NLT

You will keep in perfect peace those whose minds
are steadfast, because they trust in you.

ISAIAH 26:3 NIV

In peace I will lie down and sleep,
for you alone, LORD, make me dwell in safety.

PSALM 4:8 NIV

The LORD is my shepherd; I have all that I need.
He lets me rest in green meadows; he leads me beside peaceful streams.
He renews my strength. He guides me along right paths, bringing honor to his name.

PSALM 23:1-3 NLT

CONTEMPLATE IN PRAYER

Dear Lord,

You are the good shepherd who watches over me. Knowing You are near fills my mind and heart with peace. Because I am with You, You keep me safe from a world of trouble, so I never have to worry or be afraid.

You cover me with Your righteousness, allowing You to see me without blemish or spot. You even offer me Your calm and quiet confidence. When I hear the howls of the enemy in the surrounding darkness, I only need to turn to You and know I am safe.

The more I trust You, the more perfect my peace.

When I place my head on my pillow to sleep, I do not need to worry about all the things I've already given to You, for You are the solution to my every fear. This is why I can sleep in peace, knowing You've got a plan to turn any nightmare into sweet dreams.

For You, my dear Shepherd, provide me with everything I need. You let me rest in green meadows, and You lead me to peaceful streams so I can rest and quench my thirst. You are always ready to give me Your strength whenever I am weak. I trust You to take me down the best path for my life.

All Your gifts reflect Your care for me as well as the wonder of who You are! For You are not only my shepherd, but You are also my King. I honor You with my whole heart. Your peace surpasses all understanding and quiets my soul even in the storm.

In the name of Jesus, Amen.

REFLECT FROM YOUR HEART

1. How does this image of God as a good shepherd bring comfort to you? How does knowing that God is watching over you give you a deep sense of calm and reassurance?

2. How do the metaphors of resting in green meadows and peaceful streams illustrate God's care and provision? What are some practical ways you can rest, recharge, and find renewal in God's presence daily?

3. Psalm 23 talks about the shepherd leading his flock. How have you experienced God's guidance in your life? How does trusting in His perfect plan bring you ongoing peace and confidence?

–13–

Challenges

MEDITATE ON THE WORD

Even when I walk through the darkest valley, I will not be afraid, for you are close beside me. Your rod and your staff protect and comfort me.

PSALM 23:4 NLT

Dear brothers and sisters, when troubles of any kind come your way, consider it an opportunity for great joy. For you know that when your faith is tested, your endurance has a chance to grow. So let it grow, for when your endurance is fully developed, you will be perfect and complete, needing nothing.

JAMES 1:2-4 NLT

Little children, you are from God and have overcome them, for he who is in you is greater than he who is in the world.

1 JOHN 4:4 ESV

For everyone who has been born of God overcomes the world. And this is the victory that has overcome the world—our faith.

1 JOHN 5:4 ESV

So do not fear, for I am with you; do not be dismayed, for I am your God. I will strengthen you and help you; I will uphold you with my righteous right hand.

ISAIAH 41:10 NIV

CONTEMPLATE IN PRAYER

Dear Lord,

Sometimes the path of life makes a sharp turn into the darkest of valleys. In these shadowed places, I find myself bogged down in a dreary, relentless rain that turns my path into a muddy mess. In this downpour I can hardly distinguish the rain from my tears, and I'm wondering if I should even continue.

When I walk through these shadowy dales, I am not afraid, even when I can't see where I am going. I remember that You have never failed me before, and I trust that You will guide me now. Why should I fear when I know You are leading the way?

For when it's too dark to see, You shine the light and show me where to place my every step so that together we can climb into the beauty of the sunshine.

As I look back at my most recent trek through the dark valley, I realize that when I felt lost, You were still with me. You never left my side, because You love me and *are* my God.

You strengthened me and helped me. When the path grew too steep for me to navigate alone, You held me up with Your strong right hand so I would not fall over the cliffs. Your faithfulness is my assurance, and Your power is my refuge.

The challenges that darkened my path could not stop me, because Your light overcame the shadows.

Greater are You than he that is in the world. Because my faith remains in You, I will always find victory over my challenges. You are my strength in weakness, my guide in confusion, and my hope when I feel hopeless.

In the name of Jesus, Amen.

REFLECT FROM YOUR HEART

1. How have you experienced dark valleys in your own life? What emotions did you face, and how did you eventually find your way back to the light and God's comfort?

2. Can you recall a time when you were unsure of which way to turn, but God gently guided you? How did His loving guidance bring you peace, confidence, and a renewed sense of direction?

3. There is victory through faith. How does the idea of overcoming challenges with God's help change the way you view your struggles?

–14–

Change

MEDITATE ON THE WORD

I am going to do something new. It is already happening. Don't you recognize it? I will clear a way in the desert. I will make rivers on dry land.

Isaiah 43:19 GW

Throw off your old sinful nature and your former way of life, which is corrupted by lust and deception. Instead, let the Spirit renew your thoughts and attitudes. Put on your new nature, created to be like God—truly righteous and holy.

Ephesians 4:22-24 NLT

Brothers and sisters, I can't consider myself a winner yet. This is what I do: I don't look back, I lengthen my stride, and I run straight toward the goal to win the prize that God's heavenly call offers in Christ Jesus.

Philippians 3:13-14 GW

Trust in the Lord with all your heart, and do not lean on your own understanding. In all your ways acknowledge him, and he will make straight your paths.

Proverbs 3:5-6 ESV

Do not conform to the pattern of this world, but be transformed by the renewing of your mind. Then you will be able to test and approve what God's will is—his good, pleasing and perfect will.

Romans 12:2 NIV

CONTEMPLATE IN PRAYER

Dear Lord,

I went my own way and found myself stuck in the desert. I'm faint with thirst and I've lost all sense of direction. How did I stray so far from You?

Since I'm going nowhere, You now have my full attention. Only You can clear a way in the wilderness and guide me toward a divine turnaround.

I hear Your call to follow You and I say, "Yes."

As I change directions, I leave behind the shifting sands of my sinful past and the wastelands of empty deceptions. Lord, I open my heart to Your Spirit. Renew my thoughts and attitudes transforming me into Your likeness—righteous and holy.

I no longer conform to the world's patterns but will renew my mind with the Word of God. Now I'll be able to discern Your wonderful will for my life.

You dug me out of sand traps and made a way for me to journey through every desert. I won't look back. I'll press on, racing to win the prize of Your heavenly call in Christ Jesus.

It was good for me to come to the end of myself because it shifted my focus from relying on myself to relying on a faithful God I can trust. From now on, I will allow You to lead me as I trust You with my whole heart.

For I acknowledge that You've put me back on track and made my paths straight. In every wilderness, You are doing something new—creating rivers where there was only dry land. You remind me that You're always working, leading me forward.

In the name of Jesus, Amen.

REFLECT FROM YOUR HEART

1. Ephesians 4:22-24 and Romans 12:2 emphasize the importance of renewing your mind and putting on a new nature. What practical steps can you take to renew your mind daily? How does this renewal help you find peace and align with God's will?

2. The prayer talks about throwing off the old sinful nature. What are some habits or thoughts you need to let go of to fully embrace the new life God offers?

3. Philippians 3:13-14 encourages us to run straight toward the goal. How do you stay focused on God's purpose for your life, especially when distractions or difficulties arise?

–15–

Circumstances

MEDITATE ON THE WORD

He gives power to the faint,
and to him who has no might he increases strength.

ISAIAH 40:29 ESV

We know that all things work together for the good of those
who love God—those whom he has called according to his plan.

ROMANS 8:28 GW

Rejoice in our confident hope.
Be patient in trouble, and keep on praying.

ROMANS 12:12 NLT

This is my command—be strong and courageous!
Do not be afraid or discouraged.
For the Lord your God is with you wherever you go.

JOSHUA 1:9 NLT

Blessed is the person who trusts the LORD. The LORD will be his confidence. He will be like a tree that is planted by water. It will send its roots down to a stream. It will not be afraid in the heat of summer. Its leaves will turn green. It will not be anxious during droughts. It will not stop producing fruit.

JEREMIAH 17:7-8 GW

CONTEMPLATE IN PRAYER

Dear Lord,

Sometimes I feel stuck in a place I don't want to be. Other times, I experience one unwanted move after another, forcing me to travel in the dark. So once again, I find myself inside my moving van, traveling with no sense of direction.

As I think about what could be waiting for me down the road, I want to turn back. But You gently whisper, reminding me to let go of my fear and discouragement and to be strong and courageous. That's when I decide to let You drive because I know You have a purpose for this detour and are with me wherever I go!

My best hope is to place my trust and confidence in You. Even when circumstances uproot my life, my trust in You gives me roots like a tree planted by the water. My hope is evergreen, and I believe You will give me a fruitful harvest even in drought.

So, when my journey feels like a roaring speedway or an obnoxious traffic jam, I don't need to fret, for You are still here. You give me power and strength even when I'm running on empty.

As I trust You through the worst of times, You turn my delays into perfect timing and my every frustration into peace.

I no longer wrestle for the steering wheel as I relax into Your confident hope and joy. For now, when I think it's too dark and dangerous to move forward, I know You will guide me through my every circumstance until I find victory.

Lord, strengthen me to face challenges with courage, knowing You are always in control.

In the name of Jesus, Amen.

REFLECT FROM YOUR HEART

1. Have you ever felt overwhelmed, as though you were traveling through life with no sense of direction? How does trusting God help you gain confidence and clarity in those moments?

2. What does it mean to you to fully surrender control of your life to God? How does this act of surrender bring peace and a deeper sense of trust, especially when facing difficult decisions?

3. How does trusting God's guidance bring you a sense of victory and peace, even when the path ahead seems dark or uncertain? What can you pray to guard against fear?

–16–

Comfort

MEDITATE ON THE WORD

The Lord is a refuge for the oppressed, a stronghold in times of trouble.

Psalm 9:9 niv

When anxiety was great within me, your consolation brought me joy.

Psalm 94:19 niv

Cast all your anxiety on him because he cares for you.

1 Peter 5:7 niv

God blesses those who mourn, for they will be comforted.

Matthew 5:4 nlt

Praise be to the God and Father of our Lord Jesus Christ, the Father of compassion and the God of all comfort, who comforts us in all our troubles, so that we can comfort those in any trouble with the comfort we ourselves receive from God.

2 Corinthians 1:3-4 niv

CONTEMPLATE IN PRAYER

Dear Lord,

You are my refuge, the one who refreshes my life like a cool well on a scorching day. When I slide the well's cover aside and look into its depths, I feel its cool breath on my cheeks and anticipate its life-giving water. So, it is when I seek You during a season of pain, fatigue, and heartache.

When I slide past my barrier of bitterness, self-pity, and anger, I can experience more of You. You respond to my surrender by pouring peace into my soul and refreshing me with Your living water. The heat of my circumstances may rise, but You cool me down with joy and an unshakable sense of peace.

The more I seek Your face and give You my burdens and anxieties, the more Your peace comforts me so that I can experience Your unfailing love. You are my stronghold in times of trouble, and Your consolation fills my heart with joy and gratitude.

You comfort me even in my times of deepest grief.

I praise You for this, for the more You extend Your comfort to me, the better able I am to turn around and comfort others who are traveling down the same path of heartache I've traveled. The comfort I share with them is the very gift of comfort You shared with me.

How good it is to be loved and comforted by You in my times of trouble. I lay down my burdens and know You will carry them for me. Thank You.

Thank You, Lord, for Your love and care.

In the name of Jesus, Amen.

REFLECT FROM YOUR HEART

1. The prayer describes sliding aside barriers of bitterness, self-pity, and anger to experience God's peace. What are some barriers in your life that you need to surrender to God? How will this lead you to a deeper level of peace and freedom?

2. Have you ever experienced joy during trials? How does God's presence transform the way you handle tough situations?

3. Second Corinthians 1:3-4 speaks of comforting others with the comfort we receive from God. Can you share a time when you were able to comfort someone else because of the comfort God provided you during a personal trial?

–17–

Compassion

MEDITATE ON THE WORD

When he saw the crowds, he had compassion on them,
because they were harassed and helpless, like sheep without a shepherd.

Matthew 9:36 NIV

Shout for joy, you heavens; rejoice, you earth; burst into song, you mountains!
For the Lord comforts his people and will have compassion on his afflicted ones.

Isaiah 49:13 NIV

And he passed in front of Moses, proclaiming, "The Lord, the Lord,
the compassionate and gracious God, slow to anger, abounding in love and faithfulness."

Exodus 34:6 NIV

This is what the Lord Almighty said: "Administer true justice;
show mercy and compassion to one another."

Zechariah 7:9 NIV

Because of the Lord's great love we are not consumed,
for his compassions never fail.
They are new every morning; great is your faithfulness.

Lamentations 3:22-23 NIV

CONTEMPLATE IN PRAYER

Dear Lord,

Your heart is moved with compassion for me just as Your heart was moved with compassion for the people of ancient Jerusalem. You knew they were like sheep without a shepherd, harassed and helpless. In an act of love, Jesus, You laid down Your life for them and set them free from sin and death. Not only did You save that generation when You hung on the cross, but You also extended Your grace and compassion to me. For You are my Good Shepherd who loves and guides me through the days of my life.

Lord, Your compassion is so great that the heavens shout for joy, the earth rejoices, and the mountains sing. In Your majesty, You stoop to comfort me when I suffer.

When You met Moses on the mountaintop, You hid him in the cleft of a rock and protected him from the brilliance of Your glory. You proclaimed that You are the Lord, the Lord who is compassionate and gracious, slow to anger, abounding in love and faithfulness.

Not only do You care when I suffer, but You also want me to show compassion to the sufferings of others. As I receive Your unfailing mercy, help me reflect that same compassion to those who are hurting around me and bring hope to their hearts. Empower me daily, Lord, to be a vessel of Your comfort, spreading Your love to those who are burdened by pain and sorrow.

Thank You, Lord, that You see my suffering and are moved to comfort me through my pain. Your faithfulness and love endure forever.

In the name of Jesus, Amen.

REFLECT FROM YOUR HEART

1. Have you ever felt as if you had no shepherd, as if you were wandering without direction? How does recognizing Jesus as your Shepherd bring you peace, guidance, and a sense of security in your daily life?

2. The prayer describes Jesus being moved with compassion when He saw people's suffering. How does the realization of Jesus' deep compassion for you bring comfort and renewed hope in difficult times?

3. Isaiah 49:13 speaks of the heavens rejoicing and mountains singing because of God's compassion. How does this beautiful imagery influence your understanding of God's boundless love and care?

–18–

Confidence

MEDITATE ON THE WORD

Though an army besiege me, my heart will not fear;
though war break out against me, even then I will be confident.

Psalm 27:3 niv

In the fear of the Lord one has strong confidence,
and his children will have a refuge.

Proverbs 14:26 esv

For you equipped me with strength for the battle;
you made those who rise against me sink under me.

Psalm 18:39 esv

Be strong and take heart, all you who hope in the Lord.

Psalm 31:24 niv

For the Lord your God is he who goes with you to fight for you against your enemies, to give you the victory.

Deuteronomy 20:4 esv

CONTEMPLATE IN PRAYER

Dear Lord,

When You called me to follow You into the field, I was just a little sheep following the Great Shepherd. Little did I know that I was following You into a battlefield. It never occurred to me that You trained Your sheep for war.

The first time the enemy's arrow parted my woolly head and pierced my heart with fear, I was shocked and bleated for help, and You saved me.

It wasn't the victories of war, but the quiet assurance of Your guiding hand that taught me to be brave. Now, when the army of my enemy advances against me, my heart is not afraid, for I have confidence that You—Jesus, the Warring Shepherd—will win this battle through me. You extinguish every fiery dart from the opposing camp, and I am blessed to have Your protection. I trust in You, for You are my confidence and refuge and my unshakable stronghold against my foe.

Though it sounds impossible, You equipped this little sheep with strength for battle. You've given me courage and perseverance, and the warriors who rose against me fall away because of Your power. I will be strong and take heart because my hope is in You. I am bold because You, Jesus, have already defeated my enemy through both Your death on the cross and Your resurrection from the dead.

You, my Great Shepherd, go with me into battle to fight against my enemy and secure my victory. Your presence fills me with confidence, courage, and peace that surpasses all understanding, reminding me that no foe can stand against the power of Your eternal love and victory.

In the name of Jesus, Amen.

REFLECT FROM YOUR HEART

1. How does the idea of following Jesus into a battlefield resonate with your spiritual journey? In what ways have you felt like a little sheep facing unexpected challenges?

2. The prayer mentions feeling shocked when the first arrow struck. How do you react when faced with spiritual attacks or challenges? How does trusting in God change your response to trials?

3. The prayer talks about being confident in the face of the enemy. How do you maintain peace and courage when facing life's battles? What role does prayer play in keeping you grounded in peace?

–19–

Conflict

MEDITATE ON THE WORD

Blessed are those who make peace. They will be called God's children.

MATTHEW 5:9 GW

A gentle answer turns away wrath, but a harsh word stirs up anger.

PROVERBS 15:1 NIV

If your brother or sister sins, go and point out their fault, just between the two of you. If they listen to you, you have won them over.

MATTHEW 18:15 NIV

Then Peter came to Jesus and asked, "Lord, how many times shall I forgive my brother or sister who sins against me? Up to seven times?" Jesus answered, "I tell you, not seven times, but seventy-seven times."

MATTHEW 18:21-22 NIV

Above all, love each other warmly, because love covers many sins.

1 PETER 4:8 GW

CONTEMPLATE IN PRAYER

Dear Lord,

You have called me to turn my life into a legacy of peace in an angry world. It's hard to imagine how I could make a dent of a difference. But You bless me when I try.

You've shown me the best place to start this peace campaign is within *me*! You hone the eyes of my heart to see those who are hurting. You gently call me to respond in peace, even when others lash out in anger. You've proven that a gentle answer calms the conflict because harsh words reignite the battle.

That all seems simple enough until You give me the job of correcting my brothers and sisters. On these occasions, I humbly seek You and ask You to cover me with Your love when I point out their sin. Grant me humility, grace, and wisdom, as hiding inside Your love may be the only way to reach them. If they listen, I will have won my brother over because Your love both forgives and restores broken relationships.

You even ask *me* to forgive those who hurt me. Peter had trouble with this concept too and asked You, "Lord, how many times shall I forgive my brother or sister who sins against me? Up to seven times?" (I think Peter's suggested limit was a good idea.)

But You replied, "I tell you, not seven times, but seventy-seven times." (Which really means *always*.)

So, I yield to You and press into forgiving others, not only as an act of my will but also through the power of Your Spirit which helps me love even the unlovable.

In the name of Jesus, Amen.

REFLECT FROM YOUR HEART

1. The prayer speaks about turning your life into a legacy of peace in an angry world. What are some practical steps you can take daily to reflect the peace of Christ?

2. It's difficult to forgive the same wrong time and again, as described in Matthew 18:21-22. How does understanding God's infinite forgiveness and mercy help you forgive others, even when you've been hurt deeply and even when ongoing sin or abuse has made reconciliation impossible?

3. Matthew 5:9 blesses those who work for peace. How do you see yourself as a peacemaker? What specific challenges do you need to overcome to more fully reflect God's love?

–20–

Contentment

MEDITATE ON THE WORD

Keep your lives free from the love of money and be content
with what you have, because God has said,
"Never will I leave you; never will I forsake you."

HEBREWS 13:5 NIV

But people who long to be rich fall into temptation and
are trapped by many foolish and harmful desires
that plunge them into ruin and destruction.

1 TIMOTHY 6:9 NLT

Better a little with the fear of the LORD than great wealth with turmoil.

PROVERBS 15:16 NIV

Be joyful in hope, patient in affliction, faithful in prayer.

ROMANS 12:12 NIV

And God will generously provide all you need.
Then you will always have everything you need
and plenty left over to share with others.

2 CORINTHIANS 9:8 NLT

CONTEMPLATE IN PRAYER

Dear Lord,

Graveyards are deposits of bones, not bank accounts. If I live my whole life developing wealth instead of developing a relationship with Christ, then I could die a millionaire but not inherit eternity with You. My earthly wealth could vanish overnight, but my relationship with You will last forever. For You have promised to never leave me nor forsake me, which means my true riches are found in Your love.

Running the race to be rich can make me lose focus on the better goal of enriching my soul. Racing after the stuff that will one day fill the garbage dump will blind me to the pitfalls that could not only entrap me but also ruin my life. That's why it is better to have little and fear the Lord than to try to claw my way into great wealth that comes with turmoil.

So, my solution is to stop worrying about running the rat race if the only consolation is that I get to pack my life with stuff I don't need. A better plan is to trust You to provide for my true needs so that I will have enough to provide for the needs of others. Then, when I worship You and thank You for all You've done, I will experience a wonderful transformation. Your peace will stabilize my emotions and guard my thoughts, so I will not be stressed out over meaningless things.

Help me find contentment in Your provision and seek joy not in riches but in the lasting hope of eternal life.

I will learn how to be faithful in prayer, joyful in hope, and patient in affliction, which is not only the key to happiness but also leads to eternity in Christ.

In the name of Jesus, Amen.

REFLECT FROM YOUR HEART

1. The prayer describes graveyards as being deposits of bones, not bank accounts. How does this shape your view of material wealth? How can this awareness guide your daily decisions, especially in a world focused on accumulating possessions?

2. First Timothy 6:9 warns about the dangers of a get-rich focus. How can you guard your heart against the temptation of chasing wealth instead of developing your spiritual growth?

3. The prayer highlights how worship and gratitude can lead to experiencing God's peace. How can you make worship a more consistent part of your daily routine, even on challenging days?

–21–

Courage

MEDITATE ON THE WORD

Even when I am afraid, I still trust you.

PSALM 56:3 GW

The wicked flee though no one pursues,
but the righteous are as bold as a lion.

PROVERBS 28:1 NIV

Have I not commanded you? Be strong and courageous.
Do not be frightened, and do not be dismayed,
for the Lord your God is with you wherever you go.

JOSHUA 1:9 ESV

Don't be afraid, because I am with you. Don't be intimidated;
I am your God. I will strengthen you. I will help you.
I will support you with my victorious right hand.

ISAIAH 41:10 GW

I can do all this through him who gives me strength.

PHILIPPIANS 4:13 NIV

CONTEMPLATE IN PRAYER

Dear Lord,

I sometimes feel like a frightened rabbit who, at the first sign of trouble, dives deep into her hole. I do this because I forget that I belong to You. You have commanded me to be strong and courageous and not to be frightened or dismayed. You ask me to remember that You are with me wherever I go.

I try to calm my nerves and put on a brave face, and just when I think the coast is clear, I watch the news. Shocked by the state of the world, I dive under my couch, my newfound safe place.

But You call me out and tell me not to fear or be intimidated by the darkness. You remind me that You *are* with me. You are my God who helps and supports me with Your right hand of victory.

I'm learning to place my fear at the cross as I put my trust in You because You give me victory in whatever situation I find myself. You remind me to live my life in You so that whenever trouble approaches, I can push it back or walk through it in Your strength.

I no longer need to hide, jump at shadows, or be intimidated by the enemy because You don't see me as a frightened rabbit; You see me as a bold lion.

With Your strength, I can face challenges head-on, knowing that You've already prepared me for victory. In times of doubt, I will remember You are my source of courage and strength.

When I start to believe I can rest in Your strength, I will always be victorious in You.

In the name of Jesus, Amen.

REFLECT FROM YOUR HEART

1. The prayer contrasts the image of a frightened rabbit with that of a bold lion. What would it take to shift your mindset from one of fear to one of boldness in Christ? How can you start to embrace the boldness that God sees in you and live confidently in His strength?

2. How does recognizing God's presence help you maintain peace when confronted with troubling news or difficult situations? How can this awareness shape your response to difficulties?

3. What would your day look like if you cultivated a mindset of victory through Christ? How does this shift in your thinking bring you enduring peace, assurance, and hope, even in uncertain times?

–22–

Decisions

MEDITATE ON THE WORD

Show me your ways, LORD, teach me your paths.
Guide me in your truth and teach me,
for you are God my Savior, and my hope is in you all day long.

PSALM 25:4-5 NIV

Your own ears will hear him. Right behind you a voice will say,
"This is the way you should go," whether to the right or to the left.

ISAIAH 30:21 NLT

Commit to the LORD whatever you do, and he will establish your plans.

PROVERBS 16:3 NIV

The mind governed by the flesh is death,
but the mind governed by the Spirit is life and peace.

ROMANS 8:6 NIV

If you need wisdom, ask our generous God,
and he will give it to you. He will not rebuke you for asking.

JAMES 1:5 NLT

CONTEMPLATE IN PRAYER

Dear Lord,

Sometimes I feel like I'm strapped into skis at the top of a mountain. As I look around, I see unmarked ski trails leading in every direction imaginable. With the falling snow making visibility low, how can I know which trail to take? One trail could lead off a cliff, while another trail could lead to a dangerous ravine or impassable forest.

Your Word says You are generous with Your wisdom and will answer me without rebuke, even if I ask what I might consider to be a dumb question. So, I will trust You not to be annoyed with me, and I'll ask, "Which direction should I turn?"

As I listen for Your voice, I see Your direction is hidden inside Your Word. I hear You gently whisper inside my soul, and so I turn toward the trail I believe You've indicated.

As I tilt my skis downward, ready to plunge down the ski trail, I ask You to go before me, to lead the way. Show me Your truth, for You are my God and Savior. I will follow You all day long.

Whenever my trail becomes a crossroad, You tell me which way to turn, whether to the right or to the left.

Lord, I am committed to following You. Even if I should turn the wrong way, because I've committed this journey to You, You will right my path.

If my plans come from the desires of my flesh, I may lose my sense of direction, but when my plans are led by Your Holy Spirit, I'll find the right track. May Your Holy Spirit always be my guide.

In the name of Jesus, Amen.

REFLECT FROM YOUR HEART

1. How does this metaphor of skiing down unmarked trails reflect your feelings about making life decisions? What helps you navigate your decisions with confidence, especially when the path ahead seems uncertain or unclear?

2. The prayer acknowledges that even if you turn the wrong way, when you seek God, He will correct your path. How has God redirected your course in the past, and how did you recognize His guidance during those times of uncertainty?

3. If you need peace about decisions you are facing, take a moment to ask God for His direction and trust that He will lead you according to His perfect will.

–23–

Depression

MEDITATE ON THE WORD

Why, my soul, are you downcast? Why so disturbed within me?
Put your hope in God, for I will yet praise him, my Savior and my God.

PSALM 42:5 NIV

For I have given rest to the weary and joy to the sorrowing.

JEREMIAH 31:25 NLT

And hope does not put us to shame, because God's love has been poured into our hearts through the Holy Spirit who has been given to us.

ROMANS 5:5 ESV

He heals the brokenhearted and bandages their wounds.

PSALM 147:3 NLT

But those who hope in the LORD will renew their strength. They will soar on wings like eagles; they will run and not grow weary, they will walk and not be faint.

ISAIAH 40:31 NIV

CONTEMPLATE IN PRAYER

Dear Lord,

When I'm depressed, I stop to question myself: *Why do I feel so sad?*

I count these questions as my cue to put my hope in You. Yes, I will hope in You, and I will praise You, my Savior and Lord.

I've learned that praising You can flip the switch on my gloomy thoughts so that I can feel Your peace that passes understanding. In this moment the darkness flees, and Your light shines into the corners of my troubled mind.

I know Your arms are open wide to me, and I like to imagine I'm a little lamb and You are holding me close to Your heart, whispering words of love and care. I can imagine this because You invite me to experience Your rest when I am weary and replace my sorrow with joy.

I'm here now, and I humbly ask for Your rest. Give me the courage to let go of the burdens I cling to and trust that they are fully in Your care. When I submit to Your care, I know You will heal my broken heart and bandage my wounds.

And because my hope is in You, You will renew my strength, and I will soar out of my depression and into Your joy. I will run to You and never grow weary. I will walk side-by-side with You and never lose strength.

Because I hope in You, I will never be put to shame. You have poured Your love into my heart through Your gift of the Holy Spirit. Bless You for restoring my joy.

In the name of Jesus, Amen.

REFLECT FROM YOUR HEART

1. Think of a little lamb being held close to God's heart. How does this imagery help you connect with God's love, care, and protection for you?

2. If praising God can flip the switch on gloomy thoughts, how can you intentionally put a time of worship and praise into your day to uplift your spirit?

3. Talking to God about your feelings, giving Him your troubles, and deciding to trust Him can help you find more peace. Take some time to craft a personal prayer to talk honestly to God about your troubles and feelings. He cares deeply, and He is always listening.

–24–

Disappointment

MEDITATE ON THE WORD

Even though the fig trees have no blossoms, and there are no grapes on the vines;
even though the olive crop fails, and the fields lie empty and barren;
even though the flocks die in the fields, and the cattle barns are empty,
yet I will rejoice in the LORD! I will be joyful in the God of my salvation!

HABAKKUK 3:17-18 NLT

So we fix our eyes not on what is seen, but on what is unseen,
since what is seen is temporary, but what is unseen is eternal.

2 CORINTHIANS 4:18 NIV

"For I know the plans I have for you," declares the Lord,
"plans to prosper you and not to harm you, plans to give you hope and a future."

JEREMIAH 29:11 NIV

But blessed is the one who trusts in the Lord, whose confidence is in him.
They will be like a tree planted by the water that sends out its roots by
the stream. It does not fear when heat comes; its leaves are always green.
It has no worries in a year of drought and never fails to bear fruit.

JEREMIAH 17:7-8 NIV

Our suffering is light and temporary and is producing for us an eternal glory that is greater than anything we can imagine.

2 CORINTHIANS 4:17 GW

CONTEMPLATE IN PRAYER

Dear Lord,

You say You have plans for me, but all I see is disappointment. You say You will prosper me and not harm me, but all I feel is hurt. You say You will give me a hope and a future, but with all that's happened, how is that even possible?

Then I realize You are asking me to trust You through this disaster.

What do I have to lose?

You ask me to put my confidence in You. Okay, I will place my seedling of hope in Your hand and watch You plant it beside the still waters. As I rest in You, I feel my roots grow deep, and I start to see my past as the fodder that now helps me grow strong. Even the burning sun cannot stop me from experiencing the strength of Your love. Suddenly I feel amazing and realize I can spread my branches and bear much fruit.

But even when this season eventually changes, I've decided I will continue to trust in You. For if my fig trees have no blossoms, and there are no grapes on my vines; even if my olive crop fails, and my fields lie empty and barren; even if my flocks die in the fields, and my cattle barns are empty, I will rejoice in You! For You are still the God of my salvation, and You have a way of turning all my problems into blessings!

This is why I've made the decision to stop focusing on my problems as I fix my eyes on You. For as I trust You, I know You are turning my disasters into miracles of purpose. For disappointments are temporary, but Your ability to use them for good is eternal.

In the name of Jesus, Amen.

REFLECT FROM YOUR HEART

1. Have you ever experienced disappointment despite God's promises? What helps you maintain hope and faith during these difficult times when the outcome seems uncertain?

2. God can turn a disaster into a miracle of purpose. Can you think of a time when God turned a difficult situation in your life into something unexpectedly good or meaningful?

3. Take a moment to lift your disasters and disappointments to God and ask Him to not only turn them into blessings but to make sure you recognize that the disappointments were the seeds of a miracle in disguise.

–25–

Discouragement

MEDITATE ON THE WORD

Hope deferred makes the heart sick, but a longing fulfilled is a tree of life.
PROVERBS 13:12 NIV

Why am I discouraged? Why is my heart so sad?
I will put my hope in God! I will praise him again—my Savior and my God!
PSALM 42:11 NLT

But you, O LORD, are a shield that surrounds me.
You are my glory. You hold my head high.
PSALM 3:3 GW

But we have this treasure in jars of clay to show that this
all-surpassing power is from God and not from us.
We are hard pressed on every side, but not crushed; perplexed,
but not in despair; persecuted, but not abandoned; struck down, but not destroyed.
2 CORINTHIANS 4:7-9 NIV

May the LORD bless you and protect you.
May the LORD smile on you and be gracious to you.
May the Lord show you his favor and give you his peace.
NUMBERS 6:24-26 NLT

CONTEMPLATE IN PRAYER

Dear Lord,

I have a pretty good idea why I feel so discouraged. It's because, after much prayer, the thing I've been hoping for has been seriously delayed.

I'm starting to think it might never come to be.

If I could see my prayers answered, I know I would feel alive, like a tree teeming with life. But when I don't get what I hoped for, I wilt in the face of discouragement. That's when I must refocus my hope, not on what You will or won't give me, but on who You are.

When I shift my thoughts in this way, I can still hope in You, and I praise You in the "no matter whats." For You are my Savior and Lord, and You can turn anything around, including my attitude. (Which might be Your point.)

You are a shield surrounding me, protecting my heart. So, when I am discouraged, I know Your glory rests in me. That's why I can hold my head high as I walk past deferred hope. Even though I'm like a fragile jar of clay, You have filled me with Your love, presence, and power.

I may be hard pressed on every side, but I am uncrushable. I may be perplexed at times, but I will not despair, for my hope remains in You. I may even be persecuted, but You will never abandon me. I may be knocked down, but I will never be a cracked pot.

Even in discouraging times, You bless and protect me. You smile on me, and You are gracious to me. Please show me Your favor and give me Your peace.

In the name of Jesus, Amen.

REFLECT FROM YOUR HEART

1. The prayer talks about refocusing your hope on who God is rather than on what He can give you. How does this shift in focus help you deal with disappointment? What practical steps can you take to praise God and remain thankful, even in difficult circumstances?

2. Psalm 3:3 describes God as a shield that surrounds us. In what ways does recognizing God as your shield help you hold your head high, especially when facing challenges?

3. Numbers 6:24-26 speaks of God's blessing, protection, favor, and peace. What can you do to invite more of His peace, favor, and protection into your daily routine?

–26–

Division

MEDITATE ON THE WORD

What causes fights and quarrels among you? Don't they come from your desires that battle within you? You desire but do not have, so you kill. You covet but you cannot get what you want, so you quarrel and fight. You do not have because you do not ask God.

James 4:1-2 niv

Brothers and sisters, I encourage all of you in the name of our Lord Jesus Christ to agree with each other and not to split into opposing groups. I want you to be united in your understanding and opinions.

1 Corinthians 1:10 gw

Make every effort to keep the unity of the Spirit through the bond of peace.

Ephesians 4:3 niv

May God, who gives this endurance and encouragement, allow you to live in harmony with each other by following the example of Christ Jesus.

Romans 15:5 gw

Above all, love each other deeply, because love covers over a multitude of sins.

1 Peter 4:8 niv

CONTEMPLATE IN PRAYER

Dear Lord,

It was almost a blood bath. The bickering. The hot-headed arguing.

What was I thinking when I determined I would get my way no matter the cost? I connived, quarreled, and stood up for *me*. How could I risk allowing someone else to get what *I* wanted?

But I was in the wrong. Demanding my due is not the way You call me to interact with others. I guess I was blinded by my greed, and unfortunately, I did everything I could to win, with one exception: I did not come to You in prayer. That's why I lost my quest. I should have talked to You about the situation from the start, for You are my provider, not me. You would have helped me get what I hoped for or shown me a better solution.

But one thing I'm learning is You want me to get along with my brothers and sisters. You do not call us to duke it out, call each other names, or split into opposing groups. You want us to unite and work together. If we talk it out in love and respect, we will come to the understanding You mean for us to have.

But it takes unity through the Holy Spirit of peace before we can learn how to get along. So, Lord, please send Your Holy Spirit to empower me.

I've discovered that it also takes love to cool emotions, for love covers a multitude of sins—mine and theirs.

Lord, I need more of Your patience and encouragement so I can live in complete harmony with others with the attitude of Christ Jesus.

In the name of Jesus, Amen.

REFLECT FROM YOUR HEART

1. What if we came to God in prayer before pursuing our desires? Create a plan to make prayer your first response in every situation and note how this shift transforms your decisions.

2. Ephesians 4:3 urges believers to make every effort to keep the unity of the Spirit through the bond of peace. What is the best way to maintain peace and overcome challenges when tensions arise?

3. First Peter 4:8 highlights the power of love. How does showing love in difficult situations help to de-escalate conflict? The next time you feel annoyed, consider asking God to grant you more of His love.

–27–

Encouragement

MEDITATE ON THE WORD

But now thus says the LORD, he who created you,
O Jacob, he who formed you, O Israel:
"Fear not, for I have redeemed you;
I have called you by name, you are mine."

ISAIAH 43:1 ESV

Gracious words are a honeycomb,
sweet to the soul and healing to the bones.

PROVERBS 16:24 NIV

But encourage one another daily, as long as it is called
"Today," so that none of you may be hardened by sin's deceitfulness.

HEBREWS 3:13 NIV

May our Lord Jesus Christ himself and God our Father,
who loved us and by his grace gave us eternal encouragement and good hope,
encourage your hearts and strengthen you in every good deed and word.

2 THESSALONIANS 2:16-17 NIV

CONTEMPLATE IN PRAYER

Dear Lord,

You witnessed my first heartbeat inside my mother's womb, and You heard my first breath. You have always been with me, and You will never forget I am Yours. You know my name and have redeemed me to Yourself.

You love me and give me grace and eternal encouragement. You supply me with hope to strengthen my heart, and You pour Your love into my every good deed. You encourage me through Your Word.

Your love for me is sweeter than a honeycomb and encourages me to love others. When I share sweet words of encouragement with those You have put in my life, those words lift hurting hearts, heal souls, and strengthen bones.

Teach me how to share Your words of encouragement in a way that will help and inspire my friends and loved ones to trust You so that they can become stronger in their faith.

As I am in Your body of believers, help me to be an encouragement, and may Your body encourage me. May words of encouragement strengthen me daily so I won't turn bitter when sin tries to deceive me. When sin stings, encourage me to rise above the pain as one redeemed by Your blood and set free from darkness. Help me to shine Your light and give me Your strength through times of temptation so that others may see Your glory.

Remind me that I am Yours, fully known and loved by You, so that my life may reflect Your grace. Empower me to speak words that bring life, healing, and hope, just as You have spoken over me.

In the name of Jesus, Amen.

REFLECT FROM YOUR HEART

1. How does being reminded of God's love and redemption bring your heart peace when you are facing struggles or doubts? How does this awareness of God's love shape the way you view yourself in Christ and give you confidence in His promises?

2. How can you be more intentional about speaking words that inspire and uplift others, especially in challenging situations when people need hope the most?

3. Make a list of a few ideas of how you can encourage the people in your life who are struggling or feeling overwhelmed and how you can be a consistent source of support for them.

–28–

Expectations

MEDITATE ON THE WORD

Delight yourself in the Lord,
and he will give you the desires of your heart.

Psalm 37:4 esv

The Lord will fulfill his purpose for me; your steadfast love,
O Lord, endures forever. Do not forsake the work of your hands.

Psalm 138:8 esv

But if we look forward to something we don't yet have,
we must wait patiently and confidently.

Romans 8:25 nlt

Therefore I tell you, whatever you ask in prayer,
believe that you have received it, and it will be yours.

Mark 11:24 esv

But seek first the kingdom of God and his righteousness,
and all these things will be added to you.

Matthew 6:33 esv

CONTEMPLATE IN PRAYER

Dear Lord,

I plant seeds of Your love inside my heart, hoping for a garden of blossoms to enjoy and share with others.

Once I plant, I wait expectantly for the seeds to die so new life can sprout and break through the soil. I must wait for Your timing, for if I disturb the metamorphosis of my seeds, I could destroy their potential to bloom. This process cannot be rushed, so I ask for Your patience while I wait for my garden to grow. As I wait, I grow confident that I will see lovely bouquets of Your love brighten my future.

This waiting for my garden to sprout love is a lot like waiting on You in prayer. For I plant my prayers of hope in You, trusting that You hear me and that You will answer in Your steadfast love and perfect timing.

For my seeds of prayer will come to fruition. I know You will not forsake either me or my requests, even when I don't understand the wait. You are faithful and work behind the scenes even when I cannot see Your plan.

As the love You have planted in my heart grows, so grows my faith that You will answer my prayers. As my seeds begin to sprout, I wait in confidence for my prayer garden to bloom. I believe I will receive bouquets of answers, and these blessings will be mine to enjoy and share.

I am confident because I seek first Your kingdom of righteousness, and all these things are Your blessings for me.

In the name of Jesus, Amen.

REFLECT FROM YOUR HEART

1. Waiting for a garden to produce fruit is a lot like waiting for answers to prayer. How have you seen the fruits of your prayers over time, even if the answers weren't immediate?

2. The prayer mentions the importance of not disturbing the metamorphosis of seeds by rushing the process. How can you apply this concept to trusting in God's perfect timing, especially when you are tempted to rush ahead?

3. How does focusing on God's promises and steadfast love bring you peace while you wait for prayers to be answered? What helps you stay rooted in peace, patience, and trust during seasons of waiting?

–29–

Failure

MEDITATE ON THE WORD

The LORD directs the steps of the godly. He delights in every detail of their lives. Though they stumble, they will never fall, for the LORD holds them by the hand.

PSALM 37:23-24 NLT

For though the righteous fall seven times, they rise again,
but the wicked stumble when calamity strikes.

PROVERBS 24:16 NIV

The LORD upholds all who fall and lifts up all who are bowed down.

PSALM 145:14 NIV

But as for you, be strong and do not give up, for your work will be rewarded.

2 CHRONICLES 15:7 NIV

But he said to me, "My grace is sufficient for you, for my power is made perfect in weakness." Therefore I will boast all the more gladly about my weaknesses, so that Christ's power may rest on me.

2 CORINTHIANS 12:9 NIV

CONTEMPLATE IN PRAYER

Dear Lord,

It's a beautiful day to hike up a high mountain trail. With all the steep drop-offs surrounding me, how glad I am that You guide my every step. But even when I stumble, my hand in Yours keeps me from falling over the cliffs. Even if I should slip up, You are never impatient, but steadfast—ready to catch me and pull me away from danger. You rescue me when I call upon Your name.

I've witnessed the fall of many who refused to take Your hand. I've realized their failure could have been mine if not for my recognition of how much I need You. I ask that You give me the strength to never let go or walk away.

But even when I stumble, skin my knees, or twist my ankle and find my stride has turned into a hobble, You still hold my hand and give me the grace to continue my journey. You empower me in my weakness because Christ's power rests on me. You encourage me not to give up, promising me rewards for my work.

You remind me that my missteps can lead to greater growth because my every weakness is met with Your strength. My walk may not be perfect, but You are always with me, guiding me to victory in You.

Even in moments when I feel broken and defeated, You lift me up, reminding me that You delight in every detail of my life. Your grace is the reason I rise again with renewed strength and a heart full of hope.

I praise Your holy name.

In the name of Jesus, Amen.

REFLECT FROM YOUR HEART

1. Psalm 37:23-24 describes the Lord guiding our steps. How do you ask for God's guidance in your daily life, especially in decisions that require wisdom and discernment?

2. How does this imagery of God holding your hand to prevent you from falling help you understand God's constant protection and unwavering support during difficult times? How does it change the way you approach challenges?

3. How does trusting in God's guidance and support bring you peace, especially when the path is challenging? What helps you maintain this peace and assurance as you navigate life's difficulties and uncertainties?

–30–

Faith

MEDITATE ON THE WORD

So faith comes from hearing, that is, hearing the Good News about Christ.
Romans 10:17 NLT

And without faith it is impossible to please him, for whoever would draw near to God must believe that he exists and that he rewards those who seek him.
Hebrews 11:6 ESV

Faith shows the reality of what we hope for; it is the evidence of things we cannot see.
Hebrews 11:1 NLT

You can pray for anything, and if you have faith, you will receive it.
Matthew 21:22 NLT

For by grace you have been saved through faith.
And this is not your own doing; it is the gift of God.
Ephesians 2:8 ESV

CONTEMPLATE IN PRAYER

Dear Lord,

If Your holiness cannot abide in me because of my sins, then how can I know You?

The answer is that Your innocent Son Jesus willingly took my sin on Himself and paid for it by His death on the cross. Because of His sinlessness, Jesus was not held captive to the law of death, which He defeated when He rose from the dead.

When I heard this good news, I believed that the righteousness of Jesus covered my sins through the power of His blood. Now I can walk with You even though I am not holy enough to spend time in Your presence.

Since Your Son opened the door for me to know You, how could I miss out on the opportunity to seek You with my whole heart? You reward me by resting Your very presence in my soul.

My faith is the reality of what I hope for. It's like a rung in a ladder, a rung I hope to find as I climb in the dark. I don't fall because of my conviction that the next rung of my ladder exists whenever I lift my foot. My faith helps me trust that my next step will hold my weight. That's how I climb higher still.

By faith, I also climb a ladder of hope that leads me to Your love and forgiveness. And when I pray, I am confident I will receive what I ask for in the mighty name of Jesus. Because I can see it through You, I can receive it, not through my power, but through the power and the blood of Jesus.

Thank You for answering my prayers.

In the name of Jesus, Amen.

REFLECT FROM YOUR HEART

1. Faith is like a ladder we climb as we trust God, even in the dark. Can you recall a time when you took a step in faith without being able to see the outcome?

2. Ephesians 2:8 emphasizes that salvation is a gift of grace received through faith. How does understanding that faith is not your own doing but a gift from God change your perspective on your relationship with Him?

3. The prayer reflects on how the blood of Jesus allows us to come into God's presence despite our sin. How does this bring you peace in your spiritual journey?

–31–

Family

MEDITATE ON THE WORD

Start children off on the way they should go,
and even when they are old they will not turn from it.
PROVERBS 22:6 NIV

Honor your father and your mother, that your days may
be long in the land that the LORD your God is giving you.
EXODUS 20:12 ESV

Children, obey your parents in everything, for this pleases the Lord.
COLOSSIANS 3:20 ESV

Grandchildren are the crown of grandparents,
and parents are the glory of their children.
PROVERBS 17:6 GW

But as for me and my house, we will serve the LORD.
JOSHUA 24:15 ESV

CONTEMPLATE IN PRAYER

Dear Lord,

One day, when I look back at my family through the wise eyes of time, I will see today's future as my past. And I will know that my choice for my family and me to serve You will have paid off. For Your Word reminds me that if I start my children in the way they should go, those efforts will bless them the rest of their lives. Even if they stray, I will trust that they are in Your hands and the blood of Jesus is sufficient to save every prodigal who returns home.

Even though relationships can be complicated, I choose to honor my father and mother. I also pray that any complications that arise between my kids and me will resolve and that one day, my kids will honor me too. For You call your people to honor their parents, and You bless obedience.

But because I am not yet living in the future, I ask that You help my children be obedient, as their obedience pleases You. And one day, when my children have children, surround my grandkids with Your angels and help those sweet babies stay on Your path. For my grandchildren will be a crown of glory to me.

Help me live a life that reflects Your love and truth so my family will have a solid foundation. Strengthen our bond through You so that our home is filled with peace and joy. Help me not to spoil my children too much and give me opportunities to tell them about You and our story together. I give this quest to You, trusting You will answer with a *yes*!

In the name of Jesus, Amen.

REFLECT FROM YOUR HEART

1. It is our prayer that our children, even if they stray, will be called back to God's love. How does this prayer give you peace and hope in your role as a parent or mentor?

2. Relationships can be complicated. Stop and seek God's wisdom and guidance in resolving family conflicts and misunderstandings, trusting His ability to bring reconciliation.

3. How does trusting God with your family's spiritual journey bring you peace? Take a moment to stop and pray a heartfelt prayer to surrender your family's future to God's care, guidance, and protection.

–32–

Fear

MEDITATE ON THE WORD

But even if you should suffer for what is right, you are blessed.
"Do not fear their threats; do not be frightened."

1 Peter 3:14 NIV

But now, this is what the Lord says … "Do not fear, for I have redeemed you;
I have summoned you by name; you are mine."

Isaiah 43:1 NIV

I prayed to the Lord, and he answered me. He freed me from all my fears.

Psalm 34:4 NLT

The angel of the Lord encamps around those who fear him, and delivers them.

Psalm 34:7 ESV

Be strong and courageous. Do not fear or be in dread of them,
for it is the Lord your God who goes with you.
He will not leave you or forsake you.

Deuteronomy 31:6 ESV

CONTEMPLATE IN PRAYER

Dear Lord,

When the future seems dark and filled with danger, I peek to see if I can figure out exactly what I'm facing so I can consider my options. Should I step forward into the unknown, or should I run the other way?

That's when I recall that You ask me to be strong and courageous. You command me not to fear those who oppose me because You are with me. You remind me that You will never leave nor forsake me. These words strengthened my soul.

And yes, I understand that even though You are with me, it's still possible to endure suffering for Your name's sake. But even when I suffer for serving You or for doing what is right, You bless me. You encourage me not to fear the threats of my enemy or flee from the dilemmas I face.

When I flounder in the face of danger, I must remind myself that Your Word says, "Do not fear, for I have redeemed you; I have summoned you by name; you are mine." What a promise, a promise which gives me hope when fear shows me its fangs.

For the fear I face should not be my focus. My focus should always be You. When I seek You, You answer and deliver me.

Sometimes I wonder if fear is the real enemy I must defeat. For when I give my fear to You, then my vision clears enough for me to realize that Your angels have surrounded me, and You will deliver me Yourself.

So, I will step out in faith, trusting that You will turn my fearful situations into blessings. I will be brave in You.

In the name of Jesus, Amen.

REFLECT FROM YOUR HEART

1. Deuteronomy 31:6 encourages us to be strong and courageous because God is with us. How does this promise bring you peace, strength, and confidence when facing overwhelming challenges?

2. The prayer suggests that fear itself may be the real enemy we need to defeat. Stop and ask God to help you combat fear, keep your heart anchored in His promises, and set your focus on Him.

3. How do you practice stepping out in faith in your daily life? What fears or doubts do you need to surrender to God so you can move forward in confidence?

–33–

Forgiveness

MEDITATE ON THE WORD

Then the angry king sent the man to prison to be tortured until he had paid his entire debt. "That's what my heavenly Father will do to you if you refuse to forgive your brothers and sisters from your heart."

MATTHEW 18:34-35 NLT

And forgive us our debts, as we also have forgiven our debtors.

MATTHEW 6:12 NIV

For if you forgive others their trespasses, your heavenly Father will also forgive you, but if you do not forgive others their trespasses, neither will your Father forgive your trespasses.

MATTHEW 6:14-15 ESV

And whenever you stand praying, forgive, if you have anything against anyone, so that your Father also who is in heaven may forgive you your trespasses.

MARK 11:25 ESV

Be kind to each other, sympathetic, forgiving each other as God has forgiven you through Christ.

EPHESIANS 4:32 GW

CONTEMPLATE IN PRAYER

Dear Lord,

I'm remembering Jesus' story about a servant who owed his master ten thousand bags of gold. When the servant realized the master demanded payment in full or else planned to sell the servant and his family into slavery, the servant begged the master to forgive his debt. The master took pity on his servant and forgave him. Completely.

I would expect that the servant who had received the master's forgiveness would freely forgive others. But no.

Instead, the forgiven servant marched to the home of a man who owed him a hundred silver coins, an amount which was only a bit of jingle compared to the mountain of debt he had only until recently owed the master. The servant choked his debtor and demanded payment on the spot. The servant's debtor begged the man to be patient with him, but the master's servant would not. He threw his debtor into prison until he could pay him back.

When the servant's master heard this news, he rescinded his forgiveness toward his servant and threw him into prison for a debt he could never pay.

Lord, I can see myself in this story. You have forgiven me of a debt I can never pay too. Jesus calls me to forgive so that You, my heavenly Father, will forgive me.

So, when I stand praying, if I hold bitterness in my heart, I will forgive my debtor, so that You will continue to forgive me too.

Teach me how to be kind and tenderhearted, forgiving others as You in Christ have forgiven me, showing grace in every circumstance I face.

In the name of Jesus, Amen.

REFLECT FROM YOUR HEART

1. Mark 11:25 instructs us to forgive when we stand praying. How does unforgiveness hinder your prayer life, relationship with God, and even your relationships with others?

2. How does reflecting on Christ's forgiveness toward you motivate you to forgive others? Make a mental note to actively practice and demonstrate forgiveness in your daily life, even when it's difficult.

3. How does choosing to forgive contribute to your inner peace and emotional healing? Stop and ask God to help you forgive so you can maintain a peaceful heart when others hurt you.

–34–

Freedom

MEDITATE ON THE WORD

For the law of the Spirit of life has set you
free in Christ Jesus from the law of sin and death.

Romans 8:2 esv

It is for freedom that Christ has set us free. Stand firm, then,
and do not let yourselves be burdened again by a yoke of slavery.

Galatians 5:1 niv

So if the Son makes you free, you are truly free.

John 8:36 nlt

You were indeed called to be free, brothers and sisters.
Don't turn this freedom into an excuse for your corrupt nature
to express itself. Rather, serve each other through love.

Galatians 5:13 gw

---

*Live as people who are free, not using your freedom
as a cover-up for evil, but living as servants of God.*

1 Peter 2:16 esv

CONTEMPLATE IN PRAYER

Dear Lord,

I was chained to hopelessness, locked fast to sin and death. I was held prisoner because I was a sinner who didn't know about the Spirit of life. I'd heard Jesus came to set me free, but I was too blind to see how this news could be true.

Then I learned the Spirit of life overpowered the Spirit of death, and I dared to hope that the freedom of Christ could be mine.

I had this hope because Jesus revealed He was Your Son, Lord. I discovered He volunteered to be tortured to death to pay for my sins, the very sins I was chained to.

My blindness lifted and I saw the truth. Jesus was sinless and therefore death couldn't keep Him in the grave.

As the earth trembled, Jesus rose above sin and death and walked out of His tomb.

That's when He broke my chains and unlocked the door to my prison. I saw Him standing at the open door of my cell, and He extended His hand to me. I took it and walked with Him into the light. I knew I would be His forever.

Your Son set me free, I am free indeed.

You called me to freedom in Christ, not so that I could return to my sin, but so I could love You by serving others. I will live my life in the freedom of Christ. I will not use my freedom as a cover-up for evil, I will use my freedom to serve my Lord and Savior Christ Jesus.

Thank You for setting me free.

In the name of Jesus, Amen.

REFLECT FROM YOUR HEART

1. You were once chained to hopelessness and locked fast to sin and death. What does it feel like to experience the true freedom that comes through Christ's sacrifice and victory over sin?

2. Romans 8:2 speaks of the law of the Spirit of life setting us free from the law of sin and death. How does this knowledge bring peace, hope, and strength in times of struggle and temptation?

3. How does the reality of Jesus' resurrection empower you to live a life of freedom and victory? What does it mean to you personally that Jesus has set you free, and how does this impact your daily walk with Him?

–35–

Future

MEDITATE ON THE WORD

The Lord himself goes before you and will be with you;
he will never leave you nor forsake you.
Do not be afraid; do not be discouraged.

Deuteronomy 31:8 NIV

Yet what we suffer now is nothing compared
to the glory he will reveal to us later.

Romans 8:18 NLT

I know the plans that I have for you, declares the Lord.
They are plans for peace and not disaster,
plans to give you a future filled with hope.

Jeremiah 29:11 GW

May the God of hope fill you with all joy and peace in believing,
so that by the power of the Holy Spirit you may abound in hope.

Romans 15:13 ESV

Trust in the Lord with all your heart and
lean not on your own understanding;
in all your ways submit to him,
and he will make your paths straight.

Proverbs 3:5-6 NIV

CONTEMPLATE IN PRAYER

Dear Lord,

Today I'm facing a door that says, "Future Uncertain." My hand freezes on the doorknob and I wonder whether I should bolt the door shut or turn the knob and peek inside.

But before I fret my way into a panic attack, You remind me that I am not going into my future without You, for You are already there. You know the plans You have for me. They are plans for peace and not disaster, plans that will lead me to a future filled with hope.

So, I look at the sign on the door, and see that You've renamed it to read, "Go in God."

Oh, thank goodness! Now that's a door I want to go through, for I want to be wherever You are. Not only are You with me, but You will never leave me nor forsake me. With You by my side, why should I be afraid or discouraged?

For You are the God of hope and You fill me with joy and peace as I trust in You. Because I say yes to Your future for me, the power of Your Holy Spirit fills me with hope.

So, I step through the door to go with You, knowing even if suffering blocks my path, You will reveal Your glory as You give me the ability to endure.

This is why I will trust You with all my heart. It's so much better than trusting in what I don't understand, for Your perspective is higher than mine and You see what's ahead. I know I can trust You with whatever comes. So, I will agree to go with You, and You will make my paths straight.

In the name of Jesus, Amen.

REFLECT FROM YOUR HEART

1. Deuteronomy 31:8 reminds us that God goes before us and will never leave us. How does knowing that God is already in your future change the way you approach new challenges or unknown situations?

2. The prayer describes God renaming your door from "Future Uncertain" to "Go in God." Create a prayer that helps you trust God to believe uncertain situations are opportunities in Him.

3. Romans 15:13 highlights the joy and peace that come from believing in God. How does your trust in God fill you with joy and peace, even in difficult times?

–36–

Gentleness

MEDITATE ON THE WORD

Take my yoke upon you and learn from me, for I am gentle
and humble in heart, and you will find rest for your souls.

MATTHEW 11:29 NIV

But the wisdom from above is first of all pure. It is also peace loving, gentle at all times,
and willing to yield to others. It is full of mercy and the fruit of good deeds.
It shows no favoritism and is always sincere.

JAMES 3:17 NLT

Lead a life worthy of your calling, for you have been called by God.
Always be humble and gentle. Be patient with each other,
making allowance for each other's faults because of your love.

EPHESIANS 4:1-2 NLT

Therefore, as God's chosen people, holy and dearly loved,
clothe yourselves with compassion, kindness, humility, gentleness and patience.

COLOSSIANS 3:12 NIV

---

*You should clothe yourselves instead with the beauty
that comes from within, the unfading beauty of
a gentle and quiet spirit, which is so precious to God.*

1 PETER 3:4 NLT

CONTEMPLATE IN PRAYER

Dear Lord,

As I poke through my closet, wondering what I have to wear for the events of my life, I hear You whisper that I should wear Your yoke. Yoke? You mean like the wooden beam that connects beasts of burden together, beasts like the ox?

Wait, You're really talking to me about the burdens I already carry, aren't You? You're asking me to connect to You so You can help me carry my burdens in Your strength. For this is the way I will experience Your gentleness and sweetness of Your heart, and You will give me rest for my soul.

This will also connect me to Your wisdom which is peaceful, loving, and gentle always. You will also give me the strength to yield to others with mercy and do good deeds with sincerity and without showing favoritism.

You want my life to be filled with Your humility, gentleness, and patience, which will help me overlook the faults of others as I will see them through the lens of Your love.

When I look at the wardrobe You've provided me, I see that besides the yoke, You've given me clothes for all occasions made of the fabric of compassion, kindness, humility, gentleness, and patience woven with threads of Your love and adorned with Your Spirit.

Now when I look in the mirror, I see clothes that sparkle with beauty that comes from within me. That's because You have given me the unfading beauty of a gentle and quiet spirit, a beauty that reflects Your presence in my life, drawing others to see Your glory through me.

In the name of Jesus, Amen.

REFLECT FROM YOUR HEART

1. What does being yoked to Christ mean to you? In what ways does this partnership help you manage the burdens of life and provide you with the strength, peace, and guidance to move forward in hard times?

2. Does being clothed in compassion, kindness, humility, gentleness, and patience influence the way you interact with others, especially in moments of tension or conflict? How can these virtues help you reflect Christ's love more consistently?

3. Ask God to help you overlook others' faults through the lens of His love so that you can find peace and reconciliation in difficult relationships and maintain a spirit of forgiveness and grace.

–37–

Giving

MEDITATE ON THE WORD

Whoever is kind to the poor lends to the Lord,
and he will reward them for what they have done.

Proverbs 19:17 niv

Each of you should give what you have decided in your heart to give,
not reluctantly or under compulsion, for God loves a cheerful giver.

2 Corinthians 9:7 niv

One person gives freely, yet gains even more;
another withholds unduly, but comes to poverty.

Proverbs 11:24 niv

Give, and you will receive. Your gift will return to you in full—pressed down,
shaken together to make room for more, running over, and poured into your lap.
The amount you give will determine the amount you get back.

Luke 6:38 nlt

For I was hungry and you gave me food,
I was thirsty and you gave me drink,
I was a stranger and you welcomed me.

Matthew 25:35 esv

CONTEMPLATE IN PRAYER

Dear Lord,

I look at my bank account and worry, *will there be enough for me?* I look at my wish list and think, *I need to be more frugal if I hope to acquire all I want.* But Your Word says that You want me to be generous to others even though I'd rather be generous to myself.

But when I give to the hungry, it's like I give food to You. When I give water to the thirsty, it's like I give You drink. When I welcome a stranger in, it's like I've welcomed You. You say when I'm kind to the poor, I lend to You and am rewarded.

I don't want to miss opportunities to serve You because of a stingy heart.

But You never guilt me. You don't enjoy reluctance or want to force me to share. Instead, You hope to see me give in love, deciding in my heart what to give. You want me to be mature enough to learn how to give with joy.

Though You don't twist my arm, You have an interesting twist on the topic of giving. You tell me when I give, I will receive it back in full, even more than I gave, and the overflow will pour into my lap. You even suggest the amount I give will determine the amount I will receive from You. This is better than any investment plan. And the bonus is that my generosity will help others.

It boils down to this: the more I give to others in need, the more You provide for me. Thank You for helping me to transform my greedy heart into a giving heart.

In the name of Jesus, Amen.

REFLECT FROM YOUR HEART

1. Second Corinthians 9:7 emphasizes God's value on cheerful giving. What practices or attitudes help you cultivate joy in your acts of giving? Are there any challenges you face that make it difficult to give joyfully, and how do you address them?

2. Luke 6:38 suggests that the measure we use in giving will determine what we receive. Have there been moments when your generosity led to unexpected blessings?

3. How does giving to others bring you a sense of peace? In what ways does this peace reflect the promises of God as found in His word?

–38–

MEDITATE ON THE WORD

For no matter how many promises God has made, they are "Yes" in Christ.
And so through him the "Amen" is spoken by us to the glory of God.
2 Corinthians 1:20 niv

Let us hold tightly without wavering to the hope we affirm,
for God can be trusted to keep his promise.
Hebrews 10:23 nlt

And now that you belong to Christ, you are the true children of Abraham.
You are his heirs, and God's promise to Abraham belongs to you.
Galatians 3:29 nlt

For your kingdom is an everlasting kingdom. You rule throughout all generations.
The Lord always keeps his promises; he is gracious in all he does.
Psalm 145:13 nlt

For I know the plans I have for you, declares the Lord,
plans for welfare and not for evil, to give you a future and a hope.
Jeremiah 29:11 esv

CONTEMPLATE IN PRAYER

Dear Lord,

When I look at who You are, I can't help but notice that You are the God who not only makes promises but keeps them.

Your promises to me are amazing, like Your promise of salvation through the sacrifice of Your Son. You also promise that Your plans for my life and my future will not be filled with evil but filled with hope.

As I search Your Word, I find many more wonderful promises including promises that I can trust You, that You will provide for me, guide me, give me strength, abide with me, heal me, bless me, and give me peace, protection, and provision.

But no matter how many promises You make, I find they are all "Yes" in Christ Jesus. And in Your glory, You speak the Amen to each promise which means "So be it."

So, I will hold tightly to every promise I discovered in Your Word with unwavering hope, knowing that Your promises are for me, and You will see them through to completion.

You are faithful.

And because I belong to Christ, I am counted as one of Abraham's descendants, which means Your entire treasury of promises is mine. Thank You that I will receive each one, including my inheritance in Jesus Christ.

Lord, when my faith falters or when doubt creeps in, help me remember that Your plans for me are perfect, filled with hope, and anchored in Your love. Your kingdom is everlasting, and You keep all Your promises.

In the name of Jesus, Amen.

REFLECT FROM YOUR HEART

1. How do you hold onto God's promises during challenging times? Reflect on a personal experience where you saw God fulfill a promise in your life, and how that strengthened your faith and trust in Him.

2. Second Corinthians 1:20 reminds us that all God's promises are "Yes" in Christ. How does this assurance affect your confidence and persistence in prayer, especially when waiting for answers?

3. How does knowing that God's plans for you include welfare, hope, and peace encourage you to trust Him and walk in peace during difficult seasons?

–39–

God's Word

MEDITATE ON THE WORD

In the beginning was the Word, and the
Word was with God, and the Word was God.

JOHN 1:1 ESV

All Scripture is God-breathed and is useful for teaching, rebuking, correcting and training in righteousness.

2 TIMOTHY 3:16 NIV

For the word of God is alive and powerful. It is sharper than the sharpest two-edged sword, cutting between soul and spirit, between joint and marrow. It exposes our innermost thoughts and desires.

HEBREWS 4:12 NLT

For as the rain and the snow come down from heaven and do not return there but water the earth, making it bring forth and sprout, giving seed to the sower and bread to the eater, so shall my word be that goes out from my mouth; it shall not return to me empty, but it shall accomplish that which I purpose, and shall succeed in the thing for which I sent it.

ISAIAH 55:10-11 ESV

Your word is a lamp for my feet and a light for my path.

PSALM 119:105 GW

CONTEMPLATE IN PRAYER

Dear Lord,

In the beginning was the Word, and the Word was You. It was Your Word that called forth life. You spoke the world into existence and called the planets and stars to take their place. I can only imagine what it was like to see Your Word fling the stars into the sky. It was Your Word that caused flowers, and vines to spring from the ground and birds to take flight.

You are the Word, the Creator God of the Universe.

Not only is Your Word the source of our life force, but You also breathe life into Your Scripture, written as precious letters to me. How glad I am when Your Word speaks life to my heart, mind, body, and soul.

Your Word is how I learn Your thoughts, receive Your guidance, grasp Your peace, and train in Your ways. You use Your Word to correct and keep me on the path that leads to You as I encounter Your righteousness.

Your Word is alive and powerful. There is no sword keener than its double edge. You use the sword of Your Word to cut between soul and spirit, and joint and marrow, exposing my innermost thoughts and desires.

As the rain washes the earth, and as the snow floats from heaven, the earth receives the moisture You send. In season, the Sower spreads the seeds which sprout into a harvest, baked into bread to nourish those who eat of it. In this same way, Your Word goes out of Your mouth, not with empty promises, but with purposes for which You send it to accomplish.

Thank You for Your Word, and for Jesus, the Word of Life.

In the name of Jesus, Amen.

REFLECT FROM YOUR HEART

1. God's Word declares that it is the source of life and the force behind creation. How do you experience the life-giving power of Scripture in your daily life? Can you contemplate a moment when Scripture brought you comfort or peace?

2. Psalm 119:105 describes God's Word as a lamp to our feet and a light for our path. How do you rely on Scripture for guidance in your decisions and challenges?

3. In what ways does recognizing Jesus as the Word made flesh shape your connection to God's Word? How does this connection bring peace to your heart?

–40–

Grace

MEDITATE ON THE WORD

For sin shall no longer be your master,
because you are not under the law, but under grace.

ROMANS 6:14 NIV

For from his fullness we have all received, grace upon grace.

JOHN 1:16 ESV

Let us then approach God's throne of grace with confidence,
so that we may receive mercy and find grace to help us in our time of need.

HEBREWS 4:16 NIV

For by grace you have been saved through faith.
And this is not your own doing; it is the gift of God.

EPHESIANS 2:8 ESV

But he said to me, "My grace is sufficient for you, for my power is made perfect in weakness." Therefore I will boast all the more gladly about my weaknesses, so that Christ's power may rest on me.

2 CORINTHIANS 12:9 NIV

CONTEMPLATE IN PRAYER

Dear Lord,

The jailer chained me to my sin, tossed me into prison, and threw away the key. There was no escape and all I could do was to wait for my execution. I never dreamed You'd send Your Son, Jesus, to set me free.

How stunned I was when Jesus appeared in my cell and told me that if I believed in Him, His master key of grace would free me from my bonds.

I gladly believed. As I watched, Jesus opened the locks, setting me free from both sin and death. I had to ask Him, "Why me? With so many prisoners locked into this dungeon, why did You choose me?"

Jesus explained that even though my freedom came through the cross of Calvary, my faith embraced His grace when I chose to believe in Him. It was a simple decision to receive the grace He provided, nothing more.

Yes, I still have my weaknesses, and my enemy would be happy to slap on chains of guilt and shame, but that is impossible because Jesus' sacrifice set me free once and for all.

So, I boast in my frailties, because my Jesus is powerful enough to *keep* me free.

He continues to fill my empty cup with His power as He pours grace upon grace over me.

And even though I am a sinner, His grace, through the blood He shed on the cross, still covers my sin. Lord, that's why I can approach Your throne of grace, to receive not only more grace, but Your mercy, whenever I am in need.

In the name of Jesus, Amen.

REFLECT FROM YOUR HEART

1. This prayer talks about Jesus using the master key of grace to set you free. How do you define grace in your own words, and how has it impacted your relationship with God?

2. How does your faith in God lead to peace in your life, especially in difficult circumstances? How can you nurture this faith to experience more peace and trust in God's plan?

3. How can the grace and peace you've received from Jesus be shared with others who are still struggling with their chains? What practical steps can you take to extend grace, peace, and compassion to those around you?

–41–

Gratitude

MEDITATE ON THE WORD

Give thanks to the LORD, for he is good! His faithful love endures forever.
PSALM 107:1 NLT

Let them give thanks to the LORD for his unfailing love and his wonderful deeds for mankind.
PSALM 107:8 NIV

I will praise God's name in song and glorify him with thanksgiving.
PSALM 69:30 NIV

But thanks be to God, who gives us the victory through our Lord Jesus Christ.
1 CORINTHIANS 15:57 ESV

You will be enriched in every way so that you can be generous on every occasion, and through us your generosity will result in thanksgiving to God.
2 CORINTHIANS 9:11 NIV

CONTEMPLATE IN PRAYER

Dear Lord,

When I look online and see what my friends post, I see them living fabulous lives. That's when I stop and look at my drab and boring life. What do I have to share? Photos of my oatmeal or a video featuring my sink of dirty dishes? I guess I've turned a little green with envy, and if I'm not careful, my attitude will begin to stink.

I look at my dirty oatmeal bowl again. Thank You God that I had oatmeal. Not everyone got to eat today, but I did. And just because my friends are all smiles doesn't mean their sink is any cleaner than mine.

I realize I need to stop and count my blessings and consider all I have to be thankful for, starting with You. For You are good and Your love endures forever. In fact, Your love never fails, and You accomplish so many wonderful things in my life.

I will flip on my worship tunes and sing a song of praise as I glorify You with thanksgiving—*while* I do my dirty dishes. Oh, and thank You that I even have dishes.

I thank You that I have victory over the grump I used to be only moments ago. Thank You for filling my heart with joy and giving me a fresh attitude of gratitude.

Now I'm contemplating Your provision, I realize I have more than enough, even enough to share online. So, I join in the conversation and tell my friends how loving and generous You are to me, not to make them envious, but to share the wealth of the joys You bring.

Thanks for everything, Lord.

In the name of Jesus, Amen.

REFLECT FROM YOUR HEART

1. What daily blessings can you give thanks for today? How does recognizing even the smallest blessings lead to a deeper sense of gratitude, contentment, and peace in your heart?

2. The prayer reflects on the temptation to compare your life with others' seemingly perfect lives. How does comparison steal your peace and gratitude, and what can you do to refocus on the blessings God has given you?

3. The prayer mentions singing a song of praise while doing dishes. How can you incorporate praise and thanksgiving into your daily routine to help you change your outlook and live in a deeper, more consistent peace?

–42–

Greed

MEDITATE ON THE WORD

Do not lay up for yourselves treasures on earth, where moth and rust destroy and where thieves break in and steal.

MATTHEW 6:19 ESV

Wherever your treasure is, there the desires of your heart will also be.

MATTHEW 6:21 NLT

For what does it profit a man to gain the whole world and forfeit his soul?

MARK 8:36 ESV

For the wicked boasts of the desires of his soul,
and the one greedy for gain curses and renounces the LORD.

PSALM 10:3 ESV

Keep your life free from love of money, and be content with what you have, for he has said, "I will never leave you nor forsake you."

HEBREWS 13:5 ESV

CONTEMPLATE IN PRAYER

Dear Lord,

If what I own is all I have, then I am poor indeed. For bills evaporate riches, moths devour my clothes, my transportation will become a pile of rust, and thieves could steal all my material possessions. So, the reason I am rich is because I belong to You.

You, Lord, are my treasure; not my bank account, not a safe filled with gold, but You. For You never evaporate, never need mending, never rust, and can never be stolen from me. You are the great and mighty God, and I belong to You.

The way I look at that is this: You belong to me too. Not that I am Your owner, but I am one who loves You with all my heart. For where my treasure is, that's where my heart is, and my heart is with You, the eternal Lord of the universe.

So, what if I own the gold in every safe? If I do not have Your saving grace, I have nothing. For those who worship wealth are consumed by their love of money and will live a wasted life, even despising You and Your love.

Many among the ambitious rich will renounce You, never realizing that You are their only safe bet. It is so much better to trust You and live free of the love of money. When I do, I can be content with what You provide. Plus, I can never run out of Your love for me.

The rewards are great because one day, You will call me to pass through the veil and I will spend eternity with You.

In the name of Jesus, Amen.

REFLECT FROM YOUR HEART

1. How does the reality that bills, moths, rust, and thieves can take away material wealth impact your view of wealth and security? How does understanding the temporary nature of earthly riches help you find peace and rest in God's eternal provision and faithfulness?

2. Hebrews 13:5 encourages contentment with what you have. How does this protect you from the greed that the prayer warns against? How does practicing contentment contribute to a life filled with peace and gratitude?

3. The prayer describes God as a treasure that can never be stolen. How does viewing God as your ultimate treasure influence your priorities and provide peace in uncertain times?

–43–

MEDITATE ON THE WORD

My child, pay attention to what I say. Listen carefully to my words.
Don't lose sight of them. Let them penetrate deep into your heart,
for they bring life to those who find them, and healing to their whole body.

PROVERBS 4:20-22 NLT

Finally, brothers and sisters, whatever is true, whatever is noble,
whatever is right, whatever is pure, whatever is lovely, whatever is admirable—
if anything is excellent or praiseworthy—think about such things.

PHILIPPIANS 4:8 NIV

A good person produces good things from the treasury of a good heart,
and an evil person produces evil things from the treasury of
an evil heart. What you say flows from what is in your heart.

LUKE 6:45 NLT

Guard your heart more than anything else,
because the source of your life flows from it.

PROVERBS 4:23 GW

Create in me a clean heart, O God,
and renew a right spirit within me.

PSALM 51:10 ESV

CONTEMPLATE IN PRAYER

Dear Lord,

I must pay attention to Your Words. I cannot lose sight of them, for they penetrate my heart and bring me life and health to my whole body. Not only that, but Your Word renews my mind.

It turns out that my heart is *Your* treasure. When I receive Jesus as my Lord and Savior, Your Holy Spirit rests in me. Consequently, Your presence in my heart is *my* treasure, a treasure which I must guard with all diligence.

If I were a guard in charge of a bank vault, I would never invite a crook inside to ransack it. Neither should I open my heart to anything that would steal my peace, joy, or my hope in You. Just like a guard wouldn't pour acid on the treasures inside a vault, neither should I pour out things that would corrupt my heart which you have called me to keep safe.

The life that I have in You flows from my heart, but when I allow things that dishonor You into my heart, I stop Your flow of goodness within me.

Lord, please create a clean heart in me and renew a right spirit within me.

Instead of that which is evil, help me to think of all that is lovely, pure, right, noble and admirable, excellent or praiseworthy. For when my heart is filled with treasure like this, my life will produce good things. Otherwise, my life will produce evil because what comes from my lips flows from my heart.

Help me to entertain Your goodness so I can better enjoy Your love and mercy.

In the name of Jesus, Amen.

REFLECT FROM YOUR HEART

1. What practical steps can you take to guard your heart as you would a valuable treasure? How does guarding your heart from harmful influences contribute to your overall peace, spiritual well-being, and emotional health?

2. How does filling your heart with God's Word guard it against negativity, corruption, and the pressures of the world? What scriptures can you meditate on to protect your heart?

3. The prayer asks God to create a clean heart and renew a right spirit within you. Take a moment to do just that, then contemplate the resulting peace and renewed sense of purpose you feel in God's presence.

–44–

Guidance

MEDITATE ON THE WORD

He leads the humble in doing right, teaching them his way.
PSALM 25:9 NLT

Show me your ways, LORD, teach me your paths. Guide me in your truth and teach me, for you are God my Savior, and my hope is in you all day long.
PSALM 25:4-5 NIV

Your own ears will hear him. Right behind you a voice will say, "This is the way you should go," whether to the right or to the left.
ISAIAH 30:21 NLT

Guide my steps by your word, so I will not be overcome by evil.
PSALM 119:133 NLT

Your word is a lamp to my feet and a light to my path.
PSALM 119:105 ESV

CONTEMPLATE IN PRAYER

Dear Lord,

Here I stand at a crossroads again, knowing it matters which path I choose. One path could lead to disaster, while the other could be Your path of blessings. I pray but do not know which direction to turn. I start to panic because I want to know Your answer now. Otherwise, how will I know which path You want me to take? In my anxiety, I bark a prayer at You, "Show me now, would Ya?"

I hear the stunning silence of heaven.

Sorry!

I realize I was being demanding of You, the great God, the Creator of the universe. Who am I to bark orders at You? I bow my head and humble myself before You. Lord, forgive me. Show me Your ways. Guide me in Your truth and teach me, for You are God, my Savior, and my hope is in You all day long.

I determine to trust You, and when I do, I feel Your peace. Now I know I will not miss Your voice. For You are behind me, pointing out Your direction to me, whispering, "This is the way You should go."

Thank You for speaking to me through Your Word. Hearing You through the pages of my Bible helps me overcome the enemy's plans. Your Word is a lamp to my feet and a light to my path. You don't always use a bright high beam to guide my steps. Sometimes You use a flickering candle to illuminate my path just enough so I can see where to put my foot.

You are the light that never fails or misleads me, and my destination is always You.

In the name of Jesus, Amen.

REFLECT FROM YOUR HEART

1. Reflect on a time when you felt God guiding you as described in Isaiah 30:21. How did you recognize His voice, and how did it bring you peace?

2. Psalm 119:105 speaks of God's Word as a lamp and a light. What does it mean for God's guidance to be like a lamp to your feet rather than a bright beam? How does this metaphor apply to the gradual revelation of God's will in your life?

3. The prayer mentions humility in approaching God. How does humility affect our ability to hear and follow God's guidance, as stated in Psalm 25:9?

–45–

Hatred

MEDITATE ON THE WORD

Hatred stirs up conflict, but love covers over all wrongs.

PROVERBS 10:12 NIV

But I tell you, love your enemies and pray for those who persecute you.

MATTHEW 5:44 NIV

Don't just pretend to love others. Really love them.
Hate what is wrong. Hold tightly to what is good.

ROMANS 12:9 NLT

Turn away from evil, and do good. Seek peace, and pursue it!

PSALM 34:14 GW

For you were called to freedom, brothers. Only do not use your freedom as an opportunity for the flesh, but through love serve one another.

GALATIANS 5:13 ESV

CONTEMPLATE IN PRAYER

Dear Lord,

Ugh! That you-know-who person is at it again. No matter what I say, they take a stand against me. Their words slap me in my face, and my temper burns my cheeks.

Wow, did You see what they did, Lord? It was uncalled for. There was no justification for that. I just, I just … I just … *hate* them.

Oops. I just remembered You called me not to hate. You tell me to love my enemies.

Does that mean no matter what? Surely, You have exceptions, right?

You say to pray for those who persecute me. Why would I want to do that? You tell me to not just pretend to love others but to really love them. I'm starting to think You're serious because You ask me to hate what is wrong and to hold tightly to what is good.

I think I need to borrow Your glasses so I can start to see others the way You do—lost and hurting in a broken world.

Lord, when I ask, You set me free from hatred, and You want me to stay free. You want me to point others to Your love. So, by an act of my will, and the strength of my God, I give up my right to hate, and determine to serve those who hate me. For You, Lord, ask me to turn from evil and do good. You ask me to search for peace and keep peace.

I can only do this through Your strength, insights, and power.

I humble myself before You and say, *I'm willing. Lead the way.*

In the name of Jesus, Amen.

REFLECT FROM YOUR HEART

1. Have you ever struggled with the command to love your enemies? Why is it so difficult to love those who hurt us, and how can we apply God's command in challenging situations?

2. At times, we may need to borrow God's glasses to see others the way He does. How might God's perspective change our response to those who have wronged us and help us extend love, grace, and forgiveness?

3. It starts with a willingness to follow God's leading to let go of hating others. Are you willing to consider His call to love? Ask for God's strength to help you love your enemies and seek peace, even during difficulties and conflict.

–46–

Healing Scriptures

MEDITATE ON THE WORD

But he was pierced for our transgressions, he was crushed for our iniquities;
the punishment that brought us peace was on him, and by his wounds we are healed.

ISAIAH 53:5 NIV

Bless the LORD, O my soul, and forget not all his benefits,
who forgives all your iniquity, who heals all your diseases.

PSALM 103:2-3 ESV

My child, pay attention to what I say. Listen carefully to my words.
Don't lose sight of them. Let them penetrate deep into your heart,
for they bring life to those who find them, and healing to their whole body.

PROVERBS 4:20-22 NLT

Such a prayer offered in faith will heal the sick,
and the Lord will make you well.
And if you have committed any sins, you will be forgiven.

JAMES 5:15 NLT

He heals the brokenhearted and bandages their wounds.

PSALM 147:3 NLT

CONTEMPLATE IN PRAYER

Dear Lord,

When I imagine You pierced, crushed, and lifted on the cross, I fall on my knees and wonder, *How could they do this to You?* Then I realize, You allowed it. You allowed them to crucify You to take my place, not only for my sins but to bring me peace and to heal my wounds.

How can I thank You for these benefits? When I belong to You, You heal all my diseases as well as my broken heart. Healing my broken heart means You restore, inspire, and rebuild my hope when I suffer emotional and spiritual wounds.

But to apply Your healing touch, I need to keep Your Word before me. For the more I read and remember Your Word, the more it penetrates my heart, and the more I receive Your life and healing for my whole body.

Through Your work on the cross, I am also able to pray in faith for others so they will recover. In addition, I will experience healing and the forgiveness of my sins.

All these gifts were provided for me by Your shed blood on the cross. The power of Your sacrifice was not just a moment in time; it was a divine act that continues to transform and heal. Thank You for loving me enough to die for me. Thank You that You are alive and in me now, guiding and strengthening me daily.

Let Your life within me overflow into those around me, sharing Your love, healing, and peace wherever I go. I trust in Your power to heal every broken place in my life. May I always walk in faith, confident that Your love surrounds me.

In the name of Jesus, Amen.

REFLECT FROM YOUR HEART

1. Reflecting on Isaiah 53:5, how do you personally experience the connection between Christ's suffering and your healing? Consider the meaning of "by His wounds, we are healed," and ask God to apply this meaning to your life's circumstances.

2. Proverbs 4:20-22 encourages us to let God's words penetrate our hearts. What steps can you take to ensure that God's Word is in you? How does going deeper into the Word lead to different kinds of healing?

3. Reflect on how Christ's crucifixion brings you peace. How do you personally experience the peace that comes from knowing Jesus took your place on the cross?

–47–

Heartache

MEDITATE ON THE WORD

You, Lord, hear the desire of the afflicted;
you encourage them, and you listen to their cry.
Psalm 10:17 NIV

The righteous person may have many troubles,
but the Lord delivers him from them all.
Psalm 34:19 NIV

I waited patiently for the Lord; he turned to me and heard my cry.
He lifted me out of the slimy pit, out of the mud and mire;
he set my feet on a rock and gave me a firm place to stand.
Psalm 40:1-2 NIV

The Lord is near to the brokenhearted and saves the crushed in spirit.
Psalm 34:18 ESV

God is our refuge and strength, an ever-present help in times of trouble.
Psalm 46:1 GW

CONTEMPLATE IN PRAYER

Dear Lord,

When my life derails, and I find myself stranded in heartache, I try to drag my own emotional baggage everywhere I go. That's when I feel as though You've abandoned me. Maybe it's the tears in my eyes that have blinded me to Your presence, or maybe it's my anguish that keeps me from hearing Your gentle whispers. But the pain of feeling alone in my trials leaves me with a traumatized spirit.

But the truth is, You never abandon me. You've heard my every prayer and caught my every tear. Now I must turn to You in faith, even before I'm sure that You are with me. For when I look through the eyes of faith, I can say, "You are here."

My troubles are never overwhelming to You. I chose to be grateful in faith that You, my Deliverer, will deliver me. Now that I have the presence of mind to believe You are with me, I will wait for You, knowing You have seen my distress.

When I settle into trusting You, I start to see that You are pulling me out of my slimy pit. You set my feet on a rock so I can stand. That's when I realize this Rock is You. I am not only standing on You, but I am standing *in* You.

For You are my refuge, the place I hide when life becomes too difficult. Not only do You give me strength, but You are my strength, my ever-present help in every trouble.

Seeing You through the eyes of trust helps me rest both my trouble, as well as my troubled heart, in You.

In the name of Jesus, Amen.

REFLECT FROM YOUR HEART

1. It can be a challenge to see God's presence amid pain. Create a prayer that will help you to trust in God's presence even when you feel abandoned. Pray that prayer now.

2. How does the understanding that God is your deliverer influence the way you handle challenges and heartache? In what ways can you remind yourself of God's help and care?

3. Take a moment to reflect on the peace that comes from knowing God is your refuge and strength. Invite God to give you a deeper sense of peace through Him, even in times of trouble.

MEDITATE ON THE WORD

And I will ask the Father, and he will give you another advocate to help you and be with you forever—the Spirit of truth. The world cannot accept him, because it neither sees him nor knows him. But you know him, for he lives with you and will be in you.

John 14:16-17 NIV

But when the Father sends the Advocate as my representative—that is, the Holy Spirit—he will teach you everything and will remind you of everything I have told you.

John 14:26 NLT

But you will receive power when the Holy Spirit comes on you; and you will be my witnesses in Jerusalem, and in all Judea and Samaria, and to the ends of the earth.

Acts 1:8 NIV

In the same way, the Spirit helps us in our weakness. We do not know what we ought to pray for, but the Spirit himself intercedes for us through wordless groans.

Romans 8:26 NIV

But the fruit of the Spirit is love, joy, peace, patience, kindness, goodness, faithfulness, gentleness, self-control; against such things there is no law.

Galatians 5:22-23 ESV

CONTEMPLATE IN PRAYER

Dear Lord,

When I kneel before You, I am not kneeling to an empty religion devoid of Your presence but to the great God who created the universe, a God whose presence is with me. For when I repent of my sins and trust Jesus with my whole heart, Your Comforter, the very presence of Your Holy Spirit, comes into my being.

Even though the world cannot see Your Holy Spirit of Truth, I know Him. His power enables me to walk through every door You open in my life.

You, Father, will give me more of the Holy Spirit as I seek You—not only to guide and teach me but to remind me of the words of Jesus, which are the words of life.

It is the Holy Spirit who teaches me what to pray in times of need, even interceding for me with wordless groans. I am empowered to live a life filled with the Holy Spirit's sweet fruits—love, joy, peace, patience, kindness, goodness, faithfulness, gentleness, and self-control.

Those who do not believe in the works of the Spirit cannot understand His power. The Spirit can not only win souls, He can also empower me to overcome trials and walk boldly in Your truth.

Who can argue with the power of patience, love, and kindness? Who can arrest me for being filled with peace and possessing a gentle spirit? Who can mock faithfulness and goodness? Who can keep an argument alive when I exercise Your self-control?

No one can defeat me when I am armed with and following the power of the Holy Spirit. Thank You, Lord.

In the name of Jesus, Amen.

REFLECT FROM YOUR HEART

1. Romans 8:26 says the Spirit intercedes for us with wordless groans. What does this teach you about the influence of God's presence in your life?

2. No one can argue with our Holy Spirit's power of patience, love, and kindness. How have you seen the dynamics of these qualities in you change your circumstances? How can the fruits of the Spirit impact your life for the better?

3. If no one can defeat you when you are armed with the Holy Spirit's power, what assurances can you have as you approach your life's challenges? In what ways does the Holy Spirit bring you peace and strength in times of need?

–49–

Hope

MEDITATE ON THE WORD

As for me, I will always have hope; I will praise you more and more.

PSALM 71:14 NIV

We have this hope as an anchor for the soul, firm and secure.
It enters the inner sanctuary behind the curtain.

HEBREWS 6:19 NIV

Be joyful in hope, patient in affliction, faithful in prayer.

ROMANS 12:12 NIV

But those who hope in the LORD will renew their strength.
They will soar on wings like eagles; they will run and
not grow weary, they will walk and not be faint.

ISAIAH 40:31 NIV

May the God of hope fill you with all joy and peace as you trust in him,
so that you may overflow with hope by the power of the Holy Spirit.

ROMANS 15:13 NIV

CONTEMPLATE IN PRAYER

Dear Lord,

If a waterfall cascaded over my head, would I complain of being bone dry? But when I stand beneath a waterfall of hope, I can find myself complaining that my hope has all but evaporated.

Lord, open my eyes. Change my perspective so I can see that I am drenched in Your hope because not only are You with me, but You are also my Eternal Spring of Hope.

Your presence renews both my hope and my strength. When I feel I can't fly, You lift me up on the wings of eagles. When I believe I can't take another step, You empower me to run without weariness. And when I am weary to the point of fainting, You give me hope that refreshes my soul.

You anchor my soul to You through Jesus so I can open the curtains that once blocked me from the presence of Your Spirit and feel Your life-giving hope cascade over my soul.

You teach me to live a life free of hopelessness, for my difficulties fill me with Your joy as I choose to hope in You.

I've found hope because I trust in Your ever-present help. My troubles help me to go to my knees in prayer, and You respond by filling me with Your calm and patience.

With these daily reminders, I will always be filled with joy, peace, and trust, and my hope will overflow carrying me forward into new possibilities.

For it's not my difficult circumstances that keep me close to You, but the choice I make to hope in You, no matter what.

In the name of Jesus, Amen.

REFLECT FROM YOUR HEART

1. Reflect on Psalm 71:14 and consider how maintaining a posture of praise can help sustain hope in difficult times.

2. Have you ever allowed fear to act as an umbrella between you and God's waterfall of hope? What steps can you take to better trust God and to recognize and embrace the hope He provides?

3. If it's not circumstances but the choice to hope in God that keeps us close to Him, how do you make the daily choice to hope in God regardless of what you're facing? What difference does this choice make in your overall sense of peace and joy?

–50–

Hurt

MEDITATE ON THE WORD

The LORD is good, a refuge in times of trouble.
He cares for those who trust in him.

NAHUM 1:7 NIV

Let us then approach God's throne of grace with confidence,
so that we may receive mercy and find grace to help us in our time of need.

HEBREWS 4:16 NIV

He will wipe away every tear from their eyes, and death shall be no more, neither shall there be mourning, nor crying, nor pain anymore, for the former things have passed away.

REVELATION 21:4 ESV

He heals the brokenhearted and binds up their wounds.

PSALM 147:3 NIV

Come to me, all you who are weary and burdened, and I will give you rest.

MATTHEW 11:28 NIV

CONTEMPLATE IN PRAYER

Dear Lord,

This isn't like the time I stubbed my toe. This time I've stubbed my heart, and I'm not sure I can recover. What hurts most is how wrong this situation feels. It makes me wonder—*If You loved me the way I thought You did, You wouldn't have allowed this to happen.*

I want to turn away, but You ask me to come to You and lay down both my pain and confusion at Your feet. I can try, but I'm not sure what hurts worse—the pain I feel or the fact You didn't stop it.

Through my tears, I see You, and You speak two words to my heart: "Trust me."

"Who else is there but You?" I ask as I lay my hurt at Your feet. "You can have it—all of it."

Then I know deep within me: You're going to use this powerfully in my life as You heal my pain and tend to my wounds. You will take all my trauma and turn it into a miracle I can't imagine now. But in the meantime, I give You my pain as I find refuge in You.

I've decided to trust You and approach Your throne with confidence, knowing that You will give me mercy and grace in my time of need.

You do love me, and this tragedy does not reflect a lack of love from You. You will wipe every tear from my eyes, and one day, there will be no more death, mourning, crying, or pain. These things will pass away, but I will remain in You and in Your love.

In the name of Jesus, Amen.

REFLECT FROM YOUR HEART

1. When things go wrong, it's tempting to give God the silent treatment rather than trust Him. How do you navigate the tension between feeling hurt and choosing to trust God? What helps you move from silence to trust?

2. The prayer suggests that God can turn trauma into a miracle. Can you share a time when God transformed a painful experience into something good in your life? How can this transformation help you encourage others?

3. What does it mean for you to hide in God? How does this act of finding refuge in Him bring you peace and comfort during times of hurt?

–51–

Injustice

MEDITATE ON THE WORD

Learn to do right; seek justice. Defend the oppressed.
Take up the cause of the fatherless; plead the case of the widow.

Isaiah 1:17 NIV

Religion that God our Father accepts as pure and faultless is this: to look after orphans and widows in their distress and to keep oneself from being polluted by the world.

James 1:27 NIV

But let justice roll on like a river, righteousness like a never-failing stream!

Amos 5:24 NIV

For the Lord loves justice; he will not forsake his saints. They are preserved forever, but the children of the wicked shall be cut off.

Psalm 37:28 ESV

He has shown you, O mortal, what is good. And what does the Lord require of you? To act justly and to love mercy and to walk humbly with your God.

Micah 6:8 NIV

CONTEMPLATE IN PRAYER

Dear Lord,

Injustice is like a faucet created to deliver a flow of life-giving water, but when You turn the faucet's handle, all that comes out is a trickle of rust and maybe a dead cricket.

I do not want to live a life that draws from an empty well. Lord, it is only when You are my well that I can act justly, love mercy, and walk humbly with You, my God.

You call me to draw deeply from the well of Your love, filling my heart with compassion, courage, and a desire to reflect Your love so that I can pour Your life into others. As I do, I will learn to do right, seek justice, defend the oppressed, take up the cause of the fatherless, and plead the case of the widow.

These are real people, people who are not inconsequential to You and Your heart for justice and mercy. These are people You love, who need Your people to step up and care.

For the practice of religion that honors You, our God, is not about making ourselves feel good about the blessings You give us but about being a blessing by serving others. You are pleased when we serve You by serving widows and orphans. You are glad when we keep ourselves unpolluted by the world.

When we practice Your pure religion, the faucet of our lives will pour out a river of righteousness, like a never-failing stream bringing refreshment to a weary world and glorifying Your name in every deed.

How glad we are that our God loves justice and will not forsake His saints. We will be preserved forever.

In the name of Jesus, Amen.

REFLECT FROM YOUR HEART

1. Psalm 37:28 reveals that the Lord loves justice. How does knowing God's commitment to justice influence your perspective on the injustices you witness or experience? How does this assurance bring you peace?

2. The prayer uses the metaphor of a faucet delivering only a trickle of rust instead of life-giving water to describe the emptiness of injustice. How can you ensure that your own life draws from the well of God's love and justice?

3. If pure religion reflects service to others, especially widows and orphans, what are some ways you can actively serve those in need around you?

–52–

Inner Peace

MEDITATE ON THE WORD

You will keep in perfect peace those whose
minds are steadfast, because they trust in you.
Isaiah 26:3 niv

Therefore, since we have been justified through faith,
we have peace with God through our Lord Jesus Christ.
Romans 5:1 niv

The Lord gives his people strength. The Lord blesses them with peace.
Psalm 29:11 nlt

When a man's ways please the Lord, he makes even his enemies to be at peace with him.
Proverbs 16:7 esv

*And the peace of God, which surpasses all understanding,
will guard your hearts and your minds in Christ Jesus.*
Philippians 4:7 esv

CONTEMPLATE IN PRAYER

Dear Lord,

Peace is like floating on an inner tube down a lazy river on a hot summer's day, with nothing to think about except the music of the birds and the kiss of the breeze.

How I love it when my heart feels that peaceful. But worldly peace can capsize in an instant unless I find heavenly peace in You. To find this kind of peace, I must keep my focus and trust in You. I can't let the whirlpools of difficulties distract me from trusting in Jesus. When I stay focused on Him, I can glide through rough waters without so much as a splash.

I can have a closer relationship with You when You justify me, not through the goodness of my deeds, but through my will to repent. I need to repent even when I consider myself "good enough." For my goodness is like filthy rags compared to the perfection of Jesus—the perfection You require. Thank You that when I repent of my sins and receive Jesus as my Lord and Savior, You justify me as righteous so I can walk with You.

As I walk with You, You not only give me Your strength but also Your peace—peace that can't be stolen by my enemies. The truth is, when my ways please You, Lord, even my enemies will steer clear.

While I can appreciate the peace that comes with floating down a lazy river, I can't even begin to conceive the full beauty of the peace of God. It surpasses all understanding and will guard my heart and mind in Christ Jesus.

Lord, may I always have Your peace.

In the name of Jesus, Amen.

REFLECT FROM YOUR HEART

1. Reflect on Isaiah 26:3. How does trusting in God help you maintain inner peace? Can you recall a time when your trust in God kept you at peace during a challenging situation?

2. Proverbs 16:7 suggests that when a person's ways please the Lord, even their enemies will be at peace with them. How does living in a way that pleases God bring peace to your relationships?

3. The prayer uses the metaphor of floating on an inner tube down a lazy river to describe peace. How does this imagery resonate with your own experiences of inner peace? What are the whirlpools in your life that threaten to disrupt your peace, and how can you better navigate them?

–53–

Intimacy

MEDITATE ON THE WORD

As the deer pants for streams of water, so my soul pants for you, my God. My soul thirsts for God, for the living God. When can I go and meet with God?

Psalm 42:1-2 NIV

Draw near to God, and he will draw near to you.

James 4:8 ESV

The friendship of the Lord is for those who fear him, and he makes known to them his covenant.

Psalm 25:14 ESV

But now in Christ Jesus you who once were far off have been brought near by the blood of Christ.

Ephesians 2:13 ESV

Be strong and courageous. Don't tremble! Don't be afraid of them! The Lord your God is the one who is going with you. He won't abandon you or leave you.

Deuteronomy 31:6 GW

CONTEMPLATE IN PRAYER

Dear Lord,

The deer leaps through the mountain forest toward a hidden brook, only to discover that the hot day has evaporated her hopes for a drink. Thirsty, she searches the valley below for water, panting for a cool stream.

Like the thirsty deer, so my soul thirsts for You, Lord. My soul is dry without Your presence. Tell me, where are You hiding? How can I find You?

I have no need to panic. The secret to finding You is this: as we search for You, You draw near to us.

Now I realize that You, Lord, have been watching and waiting for me to turn my head in Your direction, and You greet me with Your love.

Your friendship is reserved for those who fear, honor, and respect You. I am one to whom You reveal Your covenant of love—how Your beloved Son shed His blood and died on the cross as payment for my sins. All those who come to You through Jesus are welcomed with open arms.

Once I was far away from You, but I have been bought by the blood of Christ.

I say yes to You and yes to Your Son. I say yes to the Holy Spirit, whose presence rests in my heart. For You are with me, and You will never leave or abandon me.

As the deer finds her cool stream, I have found You, my Lord and Savior, for You quench my parched soul. I will cling to Your presence daily, trusting that You will fill me with peace and joy. Your nearness is my greatest treasure and the source of my strength.

In the name of Jesus, Amen.

REFLECT FROM YOUR HEART

1. Deuteronomy 31:6 reassures us that God will never leave or abandon us. How does this promise bring you comfort and peace, especially during difficult times? How do you remind yourself of God's presence when you feel distant from Him?

2. How does knowing that God eagerly awaits your attention change the way you approach Him? How have you experienced God drawing near to you when you seek Him?

3. The prayer concludes with the satisfaction of finding God, likening it to a deer finding a cool stream. How do you rest in God's presence once you have encountered Him? What does it feel like to have your soul quenched by His love?

–54–

Jesus, the Prince of Peace

MEDITATE ON THE WORD

For to us a child is born, to us a son is given,
and the government will be on his shoulders. And he will be called
Wonderful Counselor, Mighty God, Everlasting Father, Prince of Peace.

Isaiah 9:6 niv

For Christ himself has brought peace to us.
He united Jews and Gentiles into one people when,
in his own body on the cross, he broke down the wall of hostility that separated us.

Ephesians 2:14 nlt

That Sunday evening the disciples were meeting behind
locked doors because they were afraid of the Jewish leaders.
Suddenly, Jesus was standing there among them! "Peace be with you," he said.

John 20:19 nlt

Now may the Lord of peace himself give you peace at
all times and in every way. The Lord be with all of you.

2 Thessalonians 3:16 niv

I have told you these things, so that in me you may have peace.
In this world you will have trouble. But take heart! I have overcome the world.

John 16:33 niv

CONTEMPLATE IN PRAYER

Dear Lord,

As I consider the night of Jesus' birth, I imagine young Mary as she looked into the face of her baby. She remembered the words of the angel who told her this baby would be great, would be called the Son of the Most High, and would sit on the throne of David forever because His kingdom would never end!

Mary surely wondered how her sweet baby could embody such words.

But because of the miracle of Jesus' birth, she knew this precious child was the gift from God that all the world had waited to meet.

As the prophet Isaiah described 700 years before Jesus was born, this child would be the "Wonderful Counselor, Mighty God, Everlasting Father, and the Prince of Peace."

So true! Jesus continues to bring us peace, uniting both Jew and Gentile into one people. His work on the cross tore down the walls that separated mankind. But it was His resurrection from the dead that truly brought us peace.

After the body of Jesus languished in the tomb for three days, He arose from the dead, walked into a room filled with His disciples, and announced, "Peace be with you."

Not only did He show His followers that He was alive, but He also announced that He was their peace, now and forevermore.

Lord, may the peace of Jesus always be with me, for Jesus has overcome the troubles of this world, indeed, the whole world. Thank You that You give me peace in every way, for Jesus is my peace, now and forevermore. He guides my steps with perfect love.

In the name of Jesus, Amen.

REFLECT FROM YOUR HEART

1. In John 20:19, Jesus offers peace to His disciples who were hiding in fear. How does Jesus' presence bring peace to you during times of fear or uncertainty? Reflect on a time when His peace calmed your fears.

2. John 16:33 reminds us that in Jesus, we may have peace despite the troubles of the world. How do you find peace in Jesus when faced with challenges and difficulties? What does it mean to you that Jesus has overcome the world?

3. How does the eternal peace Jesus offers influence your long-term perspective on life now and forevermore? How do you share this peace with others?

–55–

MEDITATE ON THE WORD

For you shall go out in joy and be led forth in peace;
the mountains and the hills before you shall break forth into singing,
and all the trees of the field shall clap their hands.

Isaiah 55:12 esv

This is the day that the Lord has made; let us rejoice and be glad in it.

Psalm 118:24 esv

You will show me the way of life, granting me the joy
of your presence and the pleasures of living with you forever.

Psalm 16:11 nlt

The joy of the Lord is your strength.

Nehemiah 8:10 niv

Rejoice in the Lord always. I will say it again: Rejoice!

Philippians 4:4 niv

CONTEMPLATE IN PRAYER

Dear Lord,

I just found an invite in Your Word that mentions You've invited me to a party. The instructions say I should go out in joy and be led forth in peace.

Wait, is this an outdoor party? I'm wondering because Your Word says the mountains and the hills will break forth into singing, and all the trees of the field will clap their hands.

Oh, I see! This joy party is a celebration of freedom. I'm glad to come.

Now I have a few questions—I have some tag-alongs who are known party crashers named Fear, Bitterness, and Worry. They've been having a party in my head for years, though not one that I've particularly enjoyed. So, would it be okay if I left them behind?

I'm going to take the freedom I feel in my heart as Your way of saying, "They are not on the invitation list."

Roger that. I also understand that though You didn't give me an exact location, You will show me the way of life, granting me the joy of Your presence and the pleasures of living with You forever. Is that correct?

I feel Your smile, and I understand that I am headed in the right direction because Your joy is my strength. So, starting this moment, I'm going to believe my strength comes from the joy You've put in my heart. This joy is more than a party favor; it's a gift from You, and I will rejoice in You always!

Yes, invitation gratefully and joyfully accepted. Consider this my RSVP. I will attend Your joy party forevermore.

In the name of Jesus, Amen.

REFLECT FROM YOUR HEART

1. What does Isaiah 55:12 mean when it talks about being "led forth in peace" and "going out in joy"? How can you apply this to your daily life?

2. Nehemiah 8:10 declares that "the joy of the Lord is your strength." How have you experienced joy as a source of strength in your life? Reflect on a time when joy helped you overcome a difficult situation.

3. The prayer describes fear, bitterness, and worry as party crashers. How do these emotions hinder your ability to experience peace and joy? What strategies do you use to leave them behind and focus on the peace and joy God offers?

–56–

Kindness

MEDITATE ON THE WORD

The LORD is righteous in everything he does;
he is filled with kindness.

PSALM 145:17 NLT

Whoever pursues righteousness and kindness
will find life, righteousness, and honor.

PROVERBS 21:21 ESV

Love is patient, love is kind. It does not envy,
it does not boast, it is not proud.

1 CORINTHIANS 13:4 NIV

So encourage each other and build each other up,
just as you are already doing.

1 THESSALONIANS 5:11 NLT

*Be kind to one another, tenderhearted,
forgiving one another, as God in Christ forgave you.*

EPHESIANS 4:32 ESV

CONTEMPLATE IN PRAYER

Dear Lord,

The fact that You are kind inspires me to ask that You fill me with kindness too so that I may reflect Your compassion and mercy in all my interactions with others.

I know Your kindness comes from Your righteousness because You are the One who has never sinned. Since I follow Jesus, I also wear His robe of righteousness. It not only covers my sins, but it also allows me to be kind to others. This is possible because I constantly experience Your love and faithfulness.

You offer me rewards when I pursue Your example. You promise I will be filled with Your life, holiness, and honor. This is such a blessing! That's why I've pulled out a pen and am asking You to help me make a list of ways I can be kind.

The first thing I realize I must do is to tap into Your empowering love. For love is patient, love is kind. It does not envy, it does not boast, it is not proud. These are gifts I will use as I practice kindness to others.

I've also realized that kindness is tenderhearted and filled with the same kind of forgiveness with which You have forgiven me. This encourages me to love my neighbor as myself, to help others in need, and to forgive my brother, even when he doesn't deserve it.

I will love others as myself and accomplish all these acts of kindness through Your power.

I've realized that a life lived in Your love will overflow with Your kindness, a kindness You call me to share with others.

In the name of Jesus, Amen.

REFLECT FROM YOUR HEART

1. The prayer emphasizes that kindness overflows from living in God's love. How do you experience God's love in a way that it naturally overflows into kindness toward others? How can you stay connected to this source of love?

2. The prayer acknowledges that kindness involves patience, forgiveness, and tenderheartedness. What challenges do you face in being kind, especially in difficult situations? How can you overcome these challenges?

3. The prayer mentions making a list of ways to be kind. What are some specific acts of kindness you can commit to this week? How can planning help you be more intentional in your kindness?

–57–

Letting Go

MEDITATE ON THE WORD

Repent, then, and turn to God, so that your sins may be wiped out,
that times of refreshing may come from the Lord.

ACTS 3:19 NIV

Do not dwell on the past. See, I am doing a new thing!
Now it springs up; do you not perceive it?
I am making a way in the wilderness and streams in the wasteland.

ISAIAH 43:18-19 NIV

But one thing I do: Forgetting what is behind and straining
toward what is ahead, I press on toward the goal to win
the prize for which God has called me heavenward in Christ Jesus.

PHILIPPIANS 3:13-14 NIV

Don't worry about anything; instead, pray about everything.
Tell God what you need, and thank him for all he has done.

PHILIPPIANS 4:6 NLT

Understand this, my dear brothers and sisters:
You must all be quick to listen, slow to speak, and slow to get angry.
Human anger does not produce the righteousness God desires.

JAMES 1:19-20 NLT

CONTEMPLATE IN PRAYER

Dear Lord,

In many an old movie, the hero tumbles off a cliff but manages to grab a branch jutting from a rocky crag. He clings to the branch as an angry bird pecks at his head. As he tries to shoo the bird away, his grip falters, and one by one, his fingers slip. He plunges into the river below, but the deep water cushions his fall. Moments later, he surfaces, gasping for air, glad to be alive!

Repenting from our sins is a lot like letting go of the branch we cling to. We hold on for dear life. But like the river saved the hero in the movie, when we let go of our sins and repent, the river of God's grace saves us. It washes away our sin and refreshes us in the Lord.

Your grace also helps me to let go of my past, for You, Lord, are always doing a new thing in my life. I trust that You are making a new way in the wilderness, filled with streams of grace that will turn my desert into a superbloom.

So, I forget my past and strain toward my future with You. I am determined to push through to my goal—the prize of eternal life in Christ Jesus.

This means I must listen for Your voice without arguing or complaining and trade my anger for Your peace. For my anger does not produce the fruit of Your righteousness in me.

Thank You, Lord, that I don't have to worry about anything. I will pray about everything as I tell You my needs and thank You for all You have done.

In the name of Jesus, Amen.

REFLECT FROM YOUR HEART

1. James 1:19-20 talks about being slow to anger because human anger does not produce the righteousness God desires. How does letting go of anger bring peace?

2. The prayer uses the metaphor of a river saving a hero to describe God's grace saving us when we let go. In what areas of your life do you need to let go and trust the river of God's grace?

3. How do gratitude and thankfulness play a role in your ability to let go of stress and worry? What are some things you can thank God for today that will help you find peace?

–58–

Loneliness

MEDITATE ON THE WORD

I am with you and will watch over you wherever you go,
and I will bring you back to this land.
I will not leave you until I have done what I have promised you.

GENESIS 28:15 NIV

The LORD himself goes before you and will be with you;
he will never leave you nor forsake you. Do not be afraid; do not be discouraged.

DEUTERONOMY 31:8 NIV

For I am the LORD your God who takes hold of
your right hand and says to you, Do not fear; I will help you.

ISAIAH 41:13 NIV

May your unfailing love be my comfort,
according to your promise to your servant.

PSALM 119:76 NIV

The LORD is close to the brokenhearted
and saves those who are crushed in spirit.

PSALM 34:18 NIV

CONTEMPLATE IN PRAYER

Dear Lord,

Sometimes my life feels like that of a lonesome traveler walking down a rough mountain trail at midnight. I worry about what lies ahead and think about the things that could be lurking in the shadows. In my loneliest moment, I say a prayer to You that lights my path with a flicker of hope. That's when I catch a glimpse of Your presence. I'm so relieved. My friend, my God, is with me.

I finally understand that You watch over me wherever I go. You are guiding me and will never leave me until You fulfill Your promises for my life. I never need to be afraid or discouraged, for there is no place I can journey where You cannot find me. You are here with me now, even as You clear the path ahead. You will never leave me.

So, when I feel alone in the dark, I realize You are holding my hand, telling me to trust You. You will help me find my footing as You lead me to the right path. In the twists and turns, with You by my side, I know I'm going the right way.

Even in dark times, You are with me. You are close to me when my heart is broken and when my spirit is crushed.

I will never give up on my life's journey, for the light of Your face illuminates the darkness that surrounds me. Your unfailing love is my continual comfort. You promise that You will always be near, turning my troubles into blessings and my sorrows into joy.

Thank You for Your presence, for I am never alone.

In the name of Jesus, Amen.

REFLECT FROM YOUR HEART

1. Do you sometimes relate to the metaphor of life as a lonesome traveler walking down a rough mountain trail at midnight? What helps you find hope and direction when you feel lost on your life's journey?

2. Have you ever had a flicker of hope illuminate a dark or uncertain time? Reflect on how this light guided you through a difficult situation.

3. How does the idea of God clearing the path ahead bring you peace? How do you trust in God's guidance when you cannot see the way forward?

–59–

Love

MEDITATE ON THE WORD

Whoever does not love does not know God, because God is love.

1 John 4:8 niv

I have loved you, my people, with an everlasting love.
With unfailing love I have drawn you to myself.

Jeremiah 31:3 nlt

And may you have the power to understand,
as all God's people should, how wide,
how long, how high, and how deep his love is.

Ephesians 3:18 nlt

Give thanks to the Lord, for he is good; his love endures forever.

Psalm 107:1 niv

And you must love the Lord your God with all your heart, all your soul, all your mind, and all your strength.

Mark 12:30 nlt

CONTEMPLATE IN PRAYER

Dear Lord,

Sometimes I feel like a pretender going through the motions of my life with no thought of anyone but myself. When my life becomes this self-centered, I realize I am like an empty shell that needs to invite more of Your love into my life.

When Your love is in my life, I reflect it to others. When I open my heart to Your love, my soul blossoms into a garden that I can harvest and share.

It's hard to understand how magnificent Your love for me is. It's deeper than the ocean and higher than the stars. Since I'm just a twinkle of life in Your vast universe, I cannot fully envision the measure of Your love. I can only ask You to help me comprehend its limitless power.

I thank You that You lavish Your love on me, for You are good, and Your love endures through all time. You ask so little of me except that I love You with all my heart, soul, mind, and strength. Empower me to fulfill this request.

To live in this depth of love, I must invite You into every moment of my life. Yes, I realize You are already here, but I'm asking that You help me realize Your presence more fully. I want to include You in my every thought as I breathe my life as a prayer of love to You.

The hope that I can better engage with Your love will be my lifelong goal and my overarching purpose. For You are love, and Your love lives in me.

Let my life reflect Your eternal love, shining through me to others daily.

In the name of Jesus, Amen.

REFLECT FROM YOUR HEART

1. How does knowing that God's love is everlasting and unfailing provide peace and security?

2. How does focusing on yourself differ from focusing on God? What steps can you take to shift from self-centeredness to living a life of serving God by loving others?

3. The prayer mentions living every moment as a prayer of love to God. How can you incorporate this idea into your daily routine? What practices help you stay mindful of God's presence and love in each moment?

–60–

Merciful

MEDITATE ON THE WORD

Have mercy on me, O God, because of your unfailing love.
Because of your great compassion, blot out the stain of my sins.

Psalm 51:1 NLT

For the Lord your God is gracious and compassionate.
He will not turn his face from you if you return to him.

2 Chronicles 30:9 NIV

He does not treat us as our sins deserve or repay us according to our iniquities.

Psalm 103:10 NIV

But because of his great love for us, God, who is rich in mercy, made us alive with Christ even when we were dead in transgressions—it is by grace you have been saved.

Ephesians 2:4-5 NIV

The steadfast love of the Lord never ceases;
his mercies never come to an end;
they are new every morning; great is your faithfulness.

Lamentations 3:22-23 ESV

CONTEMPLATE IN PRAYER

Dear Lord,

It's true we have sinned against You with both known and unknown offenses. If our known sin is on Your list of Ten Commandments, we see red flags and know we must come to You in repentance. We turn from these sins and repent. Please forgive us.

But it's the unknown sins that trap us—the nagging little jealousies we never deal with, losing our temper with our family, holding a secret grudge against the people in our lives, and choosing never to forgive those who wronged us. These are the kinds of things we'd like to ignore. But You see them, even when we don't.

I am ashamed that I haven't taken these things to You sooner. Jesus died, not just for the big sins, but also for all the little ways I fail You. I need to confess these sins and receive Your forgiveness. Have mercy on me, O God, because of Your unfailing love. Because You are the God of great compassion, please blot out the stain of my sins.

I turn to You, forgiven, so glad that You did not turn Your face from me, because You are gracious and compassionate. How blessed I am that You do not treat me as my sins deserve or repay me according to my iniquities.

Instead, You show me Your great love, for You are rich in mercy and make me alive with Christ, even though I was dead in my transgressions. After all, it is by Your grace that I have been saved.

Your steadfast love never ceases; Your mercies never come to an end; they are new every morning; great is Your faithfulness.

In the name of Jesus, Amen.

REFLECT FROM YOUR HEART

1. Psalm 103:10 reminds us that God does not treat us as our sins deserve. How does this truth impact your understanding of God's mercy? In what ways does this realization bring you peace and gratitude?

2. Lamentations 3:22-23 talks about God's mercies being new every morning. How do you embrace this renewal of mercy each day? How does this fresh start bring peace and hope into your life?

3. The prayer discusses both known and unknown sins. How do you approach God with the sins you're aware of, and how do you seek His guidance to reveal the unknown sins? How does confessing these sins lead to a deeper sense of peace?

–61–

Mindfulness

MEDITATE ON THE WORD

Be still, and know that I am God;
I will be exalted among the nations, I will be exalted in the earth!

Psalm 46:10 NIV

Search me, O God, and know my heart; test me and know my anxious thoughts.
Point out anything in me that offends you, and lead me along the path of everlasting life.

Psalm 139:23-24 NLT

For we are God's masterpiece. He has created us anew in Christ Jesus,
so we can do the good things he planned for us long ago.

Ephesians 2:10 NLT

So be careful how you live. Don't live like fools, but like those who are wise.
Make the most of every opportunity in these evil days.
Don't act thoughtlessly, but understand what the Lord wants you to do.

Ephesians 5:15-17 NLT

Do not conform to the pattern of this world, but be transformed by the renewing of your mind. Then you will be able to test and approve what God's will is—his good, pleasing and perfect will.

Romans 12:2 NIV

CONTEMPLATE IN PRAYER

Dear Lord,

It's hard to be mindful of You when I am busy entertaining my indulgences: a reel here, a clickbait headline there, and what about those YouTube shorts? Addicting, right?

But You ask me to be still and know that You are God.

This takes an action plan. I respond by turning off the noise and bowing my head as I exalt You, my Lord and my God!

I want to be mindful of Your presence, so search me, O God, and know my heart; test me and root out any thoughts that offend You. Point out everything I do that offends You as I walk with You along the path of everlasting life.

Help me read Your worthy Word while removing all my worthless influences and activities. For I do not want to conform my mind to the pattern of this world, for a worldly mind loses both its identity and purpose. That's why I will renew my mind daily in You.

Even so, it's still hard to believe that I am Your masterpiece, yet You are transforming me. And I'm starting to feel more peaceful because You've made me new in Christ Jesus. In His power, I will do all the good things You planned for me since time began.

This is imperative because I don't want to act the fool; instead, I want to be wise and do good. There is much opportunity to do good in these evil days, but I ask You, Lord, to show me which opportunities are mine. Lead me into Your purposes for my life.

Lord, in Your presence, I find peace and purpose. Help me stay mindful of Your constant guidance.

In the name of Jesus, Amen.

REFLECT FROM YOUR HEART

1. You just asked God to remove thoughts that are not based in His peace. How can mindfulness help you maintain a peaceful mind focused on God?

2. Is it a challenge to turn off distractions like social media to focus on God? What steps can you take to reduce distractions in your life and become more mindful of God's presence? How does reducing these distractions increase your sense of peace?

3. How does mindfulness help you discern God's will and purposes for your life? How does aligning with God's purposes bring you peace and direction?

Overwhelmed

MEDITATE ON THE WORD

Hear my cry, O God; listen to my prayer. From the ends of the earth I call to you, I call as my heart grows faint; lead me to the rock that is higher than I.

PSALM 61:1-2 NIV

In my distress I called to the LORD; I cried to my God for help. From his temple he heard my voice; my cry came before him, into his ears.

PSALM 18:6 NIV

When doubts filled my mind, your comfort gave me renewed hope and cheer.

PSALM 94:19 NLT

Come to me, all you who are weary and burdened, and I will give you rest.

MATTHEW 11:28 NIV

So do not fear, for I am with you; do not be dismayed, for I am your God. I will strengthen you and help you; I will uphold you with my righteous right hand.

ISAIAH 41:10 NIV

CONTEMPLATE IN PRAYER

Dear Lord,

When I am overwhelmed with issues, life, and problems, I do not need to ride in a rocket ship to find You. Nor do I need to orbit the world with a megaphone so You can hear my calls for help. For whether I'm in the pits of the earth or on the top of the highest mountain, You hear my heart-whispered prayers because You are the rock that is higher than I.

I called to You with my favorite prayer, "Help me, Lord!" and You heard me in Your holy temple. Even though I was filled with doubts, You answered my prayer with comfort, renewed hope, and cheer.

You are omnipresent, present in heaven and throughout the world, always hearing me when I call. Isaiah captured this truth: "Do not fear, for I am with you; do not be dismayed, for I am your God. I will strengthen you and help you; I will uphold you with my righteous right hand."

Not only do You hold my hand, You comfort me and calm my fears when I trust You. You promised that if I come to You with my burdens, You will give me rest.

So here I am, and I've realized that You are here too.

You are my Comforter, and You have helped me recognize that problems from my perspective are future blessings from Your perspective.

When You touch my troubles, they transform into Your solutions, and I am blessed. Not because You set me free, but because You are with me through every trouble, just as You are with me now.

In the name of Jesus, Amen.

REFLECT FROM YOUR HEART

1. The prayer mentions that God hears "heart-whispered prayers." How does this encourage you to pray more openly and honestly?

2. How does the concept of God's omnipresence deepen your understanding of His ability to be with you in all situations?

3. The prayer emphasizes that God is with us through every trouble, even if He doesn't remove them. How does this change your perspective on facing hardships?

–63–

Pain

MEDITATE ON THE WORD

But he was pierced for our rebellion, crushed for our sins.
He was beaten so we could be whole. He was whipped so we could be healed.

Isaiah 53:5 nlt

My flesh and my heart may fail, but God is
the strength of my heart and my portion forever.

Psalm 73:26 esv

We can rejoice, too, when we run into problems and trials,
for we know that they help us develop endurance. And endurance develops
strength of character, and character strengthens our confident hope of salvation.

Romans 5:3-4 nlt

Yet what we suffer now is nothing compared to the glory he will reveal to us later.

Romans 8:18 nlt

The Lord is close to the brokenhearted;
he rescues those whose spirits are crushed.

Psalm 34:18 nlt

CONTEMPLATE IN PRAYER

Dear Lord,

When my spirit is crushed, I feel forgotten by You. I feel impatient whenever I wait for You to rescue me. I even grumble at the delay.

How can I forget what You've already done to pull me out of my broken condition to bring me salvation and healing?

Two thousand years ago, I was in Your heart when You were pierced for my rebellion and crushed for my sins. You were thinking of me when You were beaten so I could be whole. You stepped into my place when You were whipped so I could be healed.

How could I be so faithless and ungrateful when You did all these things for me? Forgive me and wait with me as I await Your perfect timing. For I know You will move on my behalf when the right time comes. That moment may not come until I am finally able to trust You, even in my pain.

So, though I deal with painful days, You are still the strength of my heart and my portion forever. You not only heal my pain, but You teach me how to overcome it.

You always have a purpose for my hurts and tribulations, which gives me the courage to wear Your peace in my suffering. I can greet my trials with joy, for I know You are using them to help me develop endurance. And endurance develops strength of character, and character strengthens my confident hope of salvation.

What I endure now is nothing compared to Your suffering on the cross, nor can it be compared to the glory to come.

In the name of Jesus, Amen.

REFLECT FROM YOUR HEART

1. Romans 8:18 reminds us that present suffering is nothing compared to future glory. How does this promise help you endure current hardships? How does focusing on future glory bring you peace and hope?

2. The prayer discusses the struggle of waiting for God's rescue during painful times. How do you manage the tension between your desire for immediate relief and trusting God's timing? How can patience and trust in God's timing bring you peace?

3. The prayer talks about wearing peace in suffering. How do you consciously choose to embrace peace when you are in pain? What prayers or scriptures help you maintain peace during trials?

–64–

Panic

MEDITATE ON THE WORD

When I am afraid, I put my trust in you.
PSALM 56:3 NIV

When I am overwhelmed, you alone know the way I should turn.
Wherever I go, my enemies have set traps for me.
PSALM 142:3 NLT

I sought the LORD, and he answered me and delivered me from all my fears.
PSALM 34:4 ESV

You will not fear the terror of night, nor the arrow that flies by day.
PSALM 91:5 NIV

For God gave us a spirit not of fear
but of power and love and self-control.
2 TIMOTHY 1:7 ESV

CONTEMPLATE IN PRAYER

Dear Lord,

Sometimes I feel like I'm stuck at the top of a giant Ferris wheel. The only people who seem to notice are my fellow passengers who are trapped here with me.

Some of the riders are in tears, while others are trying to climb out of their floating chairs. Since we are stories above the earth, that's not a great idea.

To make matters worse, from my vantage point, I see a lightning storm approaching. Lord, what should I do?

Your Word says that when I am afraid, I should put my trust in You.

That may sound trite, but as I consider my options, waiting on You is my best safety precaution. Otherwise, I could panic and make choices that might lead to disaster.

You are the One with the best solutions. You even point out the traps the enemy has set for me so I can sidestep calamity.

So, when I'm caught in a place I don't want to be, I call out to You, and You answer me and deliver me from all my fears and troubles.

I have no need to be frightened—because You are with me. You have not given me a spirit of fear but of power and love and self-control. This gift of self-control means I can determine to calm down in Your strength.

Just like being stuck at the top of a Ferris wheel, when I wait on You, the storm will pass, the wheel will turn, and I will float down to safety in Your care.

Thank You, Lord, for calming my fears and leading me through every storm I face.

In the name of Jesus, Amen.

REFLECT FROM YOUR HEART

1. Review Psalm 142:3, then consider how you seek God's guidance when you feel trapped by your circumstances. How does this reliance on God's direction bring you peace?

2. The prayer uses the metaphor of being stuck at the top of a Ferris wheel to describe panic. How does this metaphor resonate with your personal experiences of feeling panicked or stuck?

3. Rather than giving in to panic, how do you remind yourself to wait for God's guidance when you are tempted to act out of fear? How has this approach led to peace in your life?

–65–

Patience

MEDITATE ON THE WORD

Love is patient and kind. Love is not jealous or boastful or proud.

1 Corinthians 13:4 nlt

Be completely humble and gentle; be patient, bearing with one another in love.

Ephesians 4:2 niv

Wait for the Lord; be strong and take heart and wait for the Lord.

Psalm 27:14 niv

A person with good sense is patient,
and it is to his credit that he overlooks an offense.

Proverbs 19:11 gw

Patient endurance is what you need now,
so that you will continue to do God's will.
Then you will receive all that he has promised.

Hebrews 10:36 nlt

CONTEMPLATE IN PRAYER

Dear Lord,

Practicing patience is like bringing a paint-by-number canvas to life. With each careful stroke, we match the numbered sections to their corresponding colors, patiently watching as a picture emerges.

Lord, like the painting, our lives can feel random until we see that You want us to fill in the empty spaces with Your love. For love is patient and kind, easy to spread across our lives. Love is not jealous, boastful, or proud but makes our lives glow. Every stroke of love we paint reflects Your grace and goodness. As we paint our life's canvas, shapes begin to emerge, but it's too soon to know what kind of picture we are creating. All we know is that we must wait for You, stay strong, take heart, and keep painting.

You call us to be humble artists, gentle and bearing with one another in love. You give us insights through our patience, and these insights help us overlook the harsh words of our critics.

When we unveil our life's work to You, we are blessed that You always kept Your promises.

As we continue to paint, a portrait of Jesus emerges. This work of art only comes as You work through our patience, faithful prayer, and careful application of Your Word. But something surprises us. As we gaze into the face of Christ, we realize this is not His portrait but a self-portrait of us. For working with patient endurance has caused us to look just like Jesus. We have grown to resemble our Master, and that was our calling all along. What a wonderful surprise.

Thank You for Your guidance, grace, and unwavering love for us.

In the name of Jesus, Amen.

REFLECT FROM YOUR HEART

1. How does the metaphor of a paint-by-number canvas resonate with your experience of practicing patience in life? How does viewing life as a work of art in progress help you stay peaceful and focused?

2. The prayer concludes with the surprising realization that the work of patience has caused us to resemble Christ. How does this awareness of growing in Christ's likeness bring you peace and fulfillment?

3. Hebrews 10:36 describes patience as the means to stay on the path toward fulfilling God's promises in your life. How does this patient journey bring peace and hope for the future?

–66–

Peaceful Heart

MEDITATE ON THE WORD

Stop all the rebellious things that you are doing.
Get yourselves new hearts and new spirits.

EZEKIEL 18:31 GW

And let the peace of Christ rule in your hearts, to which indeed you were called in one body. And be thankful.

COLOSSIANS 3:15 ESV

Create in me a clean heart, O God, and renew a right spirit within me.

PSALM 51:10 ESV

Above all else, guard your heart, for everything you do flows from it.

PROVERBS 4:23 NIV

I pray that God, the source of hope, will fill you completely with joy and peace because you trust in him. Then you will overflow with confident hope through the power of the Holy Spirit.

ROMANS 15:13 NLT

CONTEMPLATE IN PRAYER

Dear Lord,

I have been running from my fears. Even when I try to hide from them, they always find me. This is why I am afraid to approach You to claim the peace You say is mine: You are holy, while I am covered in sin. Yet You invite me to come to You, not through my goodness, but through Yours. So, like King David of long ago, I repent of my sin and ask You to create in me a clean heart and restore my soul.

As I turn from my rebellion, I turn to Jesus, the One who paid for my sins on the cross. In this exchange, You give me both a new heart and a new spirit. Thank You!

Help me guard my heart so that Your Holy Spirit will work through me. When I am filled with Your presence, it's easy to have a peaceful heart because Your peace puts my anxieties to rest. Today, I lay my problems before You with gratitude and ask for Your help in solving them. I know You hear me and are working out my problems for good.

I am thankful that Your peace is able to rule my heart. It's a peace that protects me from my fears as well as from my private war with worry.

You accomplish all this through the power and love of Jesus Christ.

Lord, You are my source and supply. You fill me with overflowing joy. You give me peace because I trust in You. You help me glow with confident hope through the power of the Holy Spirit. Thank You.

May Your peace continue to guide my heart, mind, and steps daily.

In the name of Jesus, Amen.

REFLECT FROM YOUR HEART

1. Reflecting on Psalm 51:10, how can you actively seek a clean heart before God? What specific steps do you take to renew your spirit and maintain a sense of feeling brand new? How does this renewal contribute to your inner peace?

2. Proverbs 4:23 highlights the importance of guarding your heart. What practical ways help you protect your heart from negative influences? How does safeguarding your heart ensure that peace flows through everything you do?

3. The prayer mentions running from fears but finding peace in God. How do you face your fears and anxieties with a peaceful heart? In what ways does faith help transform fear into peace?

–67–

Perfection

MEDITATE ON THE WORD

You therefore must be perfect, as your heavenly Father is perfect.
MATTHEW 5:48 ESV

As for God, his way is perfect: The LORD's word is flawless;
he shields all who take refuge in him.
PSALM 18:30 NIV

The law of the LORD is perfect, refreshing the soul.
The statutes of the LORD are trustworthy, making wise the simple.
PSALM 19:7 NIV

For by one sacrifice he has made perfect forever those who are being made holy.
HEBREWS 10:14 NIV

But he said to me, "My grace is sufficient for you, for my power is made perfect in weakness." Therefore I will boast all the more gladly about my weaknesses, so that Christ's power may rest on me.
2 CORINTHIANS 12:9 NIV

CONTEMPLATE IN PRAYER

Dear Lord,

It's hard to imagine the magnitude of Your holiness. You are the great God, who always was, always is, and is to come. You are without fault because You are perfect.

Your Son asks me to be perfect, as You are, but because I am a sinner, I blew my chance at perfection years ago. Does this mean You are too holy to walk with me?

I know Your Word is flawless, and You shield all who take refuge in You. So how can I count You as my refuge when I am flawed with sin?

Besides that, Your law and statutes are perfect and contain such great wisdom that it makes the wisest seem simple. So how can I achieve Your perfect law?

For You are holy, Your laws are righteous and refreshing for those who are holy. But because my sin leaves me unworthy, Your laws condemn me. So how can I even hope to be holy?

You understand the nature of my problem of not measuring up to Your perfection, and still, You made a way for me. By one sacrifice, You made me perfect and holy. It's mind-boggling. You, the Holy God, made a way for me, a sinner, to walk with You. You accomplished this miracle through the sacrifice of Your Son, Jesus, on the cross.

I can't comprehend the magnitude of this good news, but You reveal to me that Your grace is sufficient, and Your power is made perfect in my weakness. Therefore, I will boast even more gladly about my weaknesses, so that Christ's power may rest on me.

I rejoice that I can walk with You.

In the name of Jesus, Amen.

REFLECT FROM YOUR HEART

1. If, as 2 Corinthians 12:9 reveals, God's power is made perfect in weakness, how do you embrace your weaknesses as opportunities for God's power to work through you? How does this perspective bring you peace during times when you feel weak?

2. How do you rely on God's grace as sufficient when you feel inadequate or unworthy? How does this reliance help you find peace in your spiritual journey?

3. How do you experience joy in your relationship with God, knowing that He walks with you despite your flaws? How does the knowledge that God stays with you bring lasting peace and fulfillment?

–68–

Prayer

MEDITATE ON THE WORD

Then you will call on me and come and pray to me, and I will listen to you.

JEREMIAH 29:12 NIV

Devote yourselves to prayer, being watchful and thankful.

COLOSSIANS 4:2 NIV

Confess your sins to each other and pray for each other so that you may be healed. The earnest prayer of a righteous person has great power and produces wonderful results.

JAMES 5:16 NLT

Rejoice always, pray continually, give thanks in all circumstances; for this is God's will for you in Christ Jesus.

1 THESSALONIANS 5:16-18 NIV

Don't worry about anything; instead, pray about everything. Tell God what you need, and thank him for all he has done.

PHILIPPIANS 4:6 NLT

CONTEMPLATE IN PRAYER

Dear Lord,

So many people have no clue about this thing called prayer. They don't realize they can talk to You and bring You their praises, burdens, and requests. People are often afraid of offending You, so they don't even try to pray, fearing they'll do it wrong.

But prayer is a wonderful way to grow in my relationship with You because You want me to talk to You. You care about what I have to say, and You listen when I pray. You also want me to hear Your voice through reading Your Word.

I love the Apostle Paul's recipe for prayer: First, I tell You what I need, and You supply the ingredients. Then, I add a cup of thanks and stir my prayer continually to You.

Jesus Himself loved to pray. Late at night, He'd slip away from the crowds to talk to You, His heavenly Father. So, if Jesus prayed to You, then so will I. I will also remain watchful for the enemy's traps and stay grateful for Your guidance.

James, the disciple and brother of Jesus, encouraged us to pray for one another so that we may be healed. He reminded us that our heartfelt prayers carry great power and produce wonderful results.

So, because I know You are moved by my prayers, I pray for all the people You have placed in my life, asking for their healing.

As I remain in continual prayer, I rejoice and thank You for all my circumstances, as this is Your will for me in Christ Jesus. Thank You.

Help me cultivate a deeper prayer life filled with faith and perseverance.

In the name of Jesus, Amen.

REFLECT FROM YOUR HEART

1. Philippians 4:6 encourages us to pray about everything. How do you replace worry with prayer in your daily life? Take a moment to thank God in advance for how He will transform your difficulties into blessings.

2. If Jesus took time to slip away and pray, how can you carve out moments in your day to follow His example?

3. The prayer concludes with a focus on always rejoicing and thanking God in all circumstances. If you commit to practicing gratitude in your prayers, even during difficult times, how might this help you find deeper peace and trust in God's plan for your life?

–69–

Protection

MEDITATE ON THE WORD

He will cover you with his feathers, and under his wings you will find refuge;
his faithfulness will be your shield and rampart.

PSALM 91:4 NIV

The LORD is my rock, my fortress and my deliverer; my God is my rock,
in whom I take refuge, my shield and the horn of my salvation, my stronghold.

PSALM 18:2 NIV

The LORD will keep you from all harm—he will watch over your life.

PSALM 121:7 NIV

The Lord is faithful, and he will strengthen you and protect you from the evil one.

2 THESSALONIANS 3:3 NIV

God is our refuge and strength, an ever-present help in trouble.

PSALM 46:1 NIV

CONTEMPLATE IN PRAYER

Dear Lord,

It's the dead of night when I receive the news—news that descends around me like missiles from a midnight sky. I hear the whine of their approach, and my world quakes at their impact. I have nowhere to turn, no place to hide, no safe refuge—except in You.

For You, my God, are my refuge and strength. You are my ever-present help in times of trouble. As the Psalmist said, in times of trouble, You will cover me with Your feathers and hide me beneath Your wings. Your faithfulness will be my shield, my wall of protection.

And I know from experience, as David declared, that the Lord is our unshakable foundation, our protector in times of trouble, and the source of our strength and deliverance.

So often, I have hidden in You, knowing I am safe from the enemy's attack.

No one ever wishes for their world to fall apart, but if the unthinkable comes to my door, I know You will keep me from harm as You watch over my life.

Thank You, Lord, for Your faithfulness. Thank You for giving me strength and protecting me from the evil one.

For after any nightmare, the dawn of a new day comes, and I will find You there. Whether the nightmare was only a dream or my new reality, You will walk with me into the day. You will protect me and stand by my side. Nightmares may come, but even then, You will never leave me. You will see me through.

How blessed I am to know You are near.

In the name of Jesus, Amen.

REFLECT FROM YOUR HEART

1. Second Thessalonians 3:3 speaks of God's faithfulness in protecting us from the evil one. How does this protection give you peace and confidence to face spiritual battles?

2. The metaphor of the missiles falling in the night describes unexpected bad news or crises. How does this metaphor resonate with your personal experiences? When life's challenges feel like a sudden attack, what can you pray to help you find peace and refuge in God?

3. God is faithful and will go with you when you have a life-changing nightmare. How do you hold onto God's faithfulness when you wake up to new challenges? How does this ongoing presence of God in your life bring you peace and hope?

Provision

MEDITATE ON THE WORD

He provides food for those who fear him;
he remembers his covenant forever.

Psalm 111:5 NIV

The lions may grow weak and hungry,
but those who seek the Lord lack no good thing.

Psalm 34:10 NIV

And my God will meet all your needs
according to the riches of his glory in Christ Jesus.

Philippians 4:19 NIV

The generous will themselves be blessed,
for they share their food with the poor.

Proverbs 22:9 NIV

Look at the birds of the air;
they do not sow or reap or store away in barns,
and yet your heavenly Father feeds them.
Are you not much more valuable than they?

Matthew 6:26 NIV

CONTEMPLATE IN PRAYER

Dear Lord,

You're the owner of all the universe and the creator of every resource. You provide for me as you provide for the birds of the air. They do not sow or reap or store away in barns, and yet You, my heavenly provider, feed them too. And though You care about the birds, You care even more for me and are deeply invested in my finances and needs.

With this in mind, I know that whenever I have a need, I can trust You to provide. You are the One who provides food for those who fear You and remembers those with whom You are in covenant.

Even if lions go hungry, I will continue to seek You, and I will lack no good thing.

Who could ask for a better financial plan than that?

Well, as it turns out—a lot of people rely on Your provision! I'm not the only one who recognizes that You are the ultimate provider. You meet all our needs according to the riches of Your glory in Christ Jesus.

Because of this, I have the confidence to be generous to others in need. I know that when I take care of others, I am imitating Your generosity and goodness. While I should be wise with the resources You've given me, I don't need to hoard them for fear of shortage. You always give what is good for me—whether it is plenty so I can share with others or scarcity so I must depend more closely upon You.

Thank You, Lord, for taking such good care of me.

In the name of Jesus, Amen.

REFLECT FROM YOUR HEART

1. According to Psalm 34:10, those who seek the Lord lack no good thing, even when lions may grow weak and hungry. How have you seen God provide for you in times of need? How does this experience strengthen your peace and confidence in God's provision?

2. The prayer mentions trusting God with financial provision. How do you maintain your faith in God's provision during economic challenges? How does this faith sustain your peace in uncertain times?

3. If sharing with the poor is a way to celebrate God's provision and to express our trust in Him, how do you incorporate this practice into your life? How does this act of sharing bring you peace and a deeper connection with God's generosity?

–71–

Redemption

MEDITATE ON THE WORD

For the wages of sin is death, but the free gift of God is eternal life through Christ Jesus our Lord.

ROMANS 6:23 NLT

But God demonstrates his own love for us in this: While we were still sinners, Christ died for us.

ROMANS 5:8 NIV

For you know that God paid a ransom to save you from the empty life you inherited from your ancestors. And it was not paid with mere gold or silver, which lose their value. It was the precious blood of Christ, the sinless, spotless Lamb of God.

1 PETER 1:18-19 NLT

He canceled the record of the charges against us and took it away by nailing it to the cross.

COLOSSIANS 2:14 NLT

But now in Christ Jesus you who once were far away have been brought near by the blood of Christ.

EPHESIANS 2:13 NIV

CONTEMPLATE IN PRAYER

Dear Lord,

If a game show host told me I'd won the chance to choose a prize by picking either door number one or door number two, I'd be thrilled. But what if he said, "There's a catch. One door leads to eternal life, and the other door leads to death."

I would say, "Excuse me? Would you mind telling me which door is which?"

The host might look at me as if I had two heads and say, "Can't you read?"

I'd see that the sign on door number two is labeled in large letters, "SIN." Then I'd squint at door number one and see a name written in tiny print. "What does it say?" I'd ask.

The host would stare back. "Jesus—can't you see Him?"

Of course! My sin will lead me to death, but Lord, Your free gift of eternal life comes through Jesus Christ.

Knowing the secret of the two doors makes my decision a no-brainer—it's door number one all the way. For You, Lord, demonstrated Your love for me when You sent Jesus to die for me, even though I was a sinner. You paid a ransom to save me from my empty life, which I inherited from my ancestors. Your ransom for my life was more costly than silver or gold; it was the precious blood of Christ, Your sinless, spotless Lamb.

Jesus canceled the record of the charges against me when He allowed the Roman guards to nail Him to the cross. So now, when I pick the door labeled "Jesus," the blood of Jesus pays the price for my sin so that I can enter eternity with Christ.

In the name of Jesus, Amen.

REFLECT FROM YOUR HEART

1. The prayer uses the metaphor of two doors: one leading to sin and death, the other to Jesus and eternal life. How does this metaphor help you make daily decisions that honor God? How does choosing door number one bring peace into your life?

2. Romans 5:8 tells us that God loved us even while we were still sinners. How does this truth encourage you to find peace in God's unconditional love?

3. According to 1 Peter 1:18-19, God saved us from an empty life. In what ways have you seen or experienced God filling the emptiness in your life? How does this transformation contribute to your sense of peace?

–72–

MEDITATE ON THE WORD

He saved us, not because of righteous things we had done, but because of his mercy. He saved us through the washing of rebirth and renewal by the Holy Spirit.

Titus 3:5 niv

Throw off your old sinful nature and your former way of life, which is corrupted by lust and deception. Instead, let the Spirit renew your thoughts and attitudes. Put on your new nature, created to be like God—truly righteous and holy.

Ephesians 4:22-24 nlt

Therefore, if anyone is in Christ, the new creation has come: The old has gone, the new is here!

2 Corinthians 5:17 niv

Don't copy the behavior and customs of this world, but let God transform you into a new person by changing the way you think. Then you will learn to know God's will for you, which is good and pleasing and perfect.

Romans 12:2 nlt

Create in me a pure heart, O God,
and renew a steadfast spirit within me.

Psalm 51:10 niv

CONTEMPLATE IN PRAYER

Dear Lord,

I'm thinking of a story from Your Word about King David. He stood on his roof late one evening and saw the lovely Bathsheba in her bath. He sent for her to come to the palace, and soon she was pregnant with his child. The trouble was, she was the wife of Uriah, one of his most loyal soldiers.

To cover his sin, David summoned Uriah home, hoping he would sleep with his wife. When Uriah refused, David ordered him to the front lines to ensure his death. David soon found himself guilty of both adultery and murder. David's terrible deeds were discovered, and his heart was broken with shame. He deeply repented before You.

Lord, like David, I have also sinned against You and am overwhelmed by the weight of my own failings. I ask You now to create in me a pure heart and renew a right spirit within me.

And because of Your mercy, You do! You wash away my sins and renew me with Your Holy Spirit. I am a new creation. The old has gone, the new is here. I have thrown off both my sinful nature and my former way of life, which was corrupted by lust and deception.

Lord, Your Spirit renews my thoughts and changes my attitude. I put on my new nature, which makes me like You—righteous and holy.

I will no longer conform to the customs of this world but allow You to transform me into a new person, changing the way I think. Now I can follow Your peace, seek Your will for me, and obey You in doing what is good and pleasing in Your sight.

In the name of Jesus, Amen.

REFLECT FROM YOUR HEART

1. David's story of sin and repentance is a powerful example of seeking God's renewal. How does David's prayer for a pure heart resonate with your own experiences of seeking forgiveness and renewal? How does this process lead to peace?

2. Reflecting on Ephesians 4:22-24, what are some specific old thoughts and attitudes that you need to throw off? How does adopting a new nature in Christ lead to inner peace?

3. Romans 12:2 speaks of being transformed by the renewing of your mind. How does renewing your mind through Scripture help you to resist conforming to the world? How does this transformation contribute to your peace?

–73–

Repentance

MEDITATE ON THE WORD

Repent, then, and turn to God, so that your sins may be wiped out,
that times of refreshing may come from the Lord.

Acts 3:19 NIV

The Lord is not slow in keeping his promise, as some understand slowness.
Instead he is patient with you, not wanting anyone to perish,
but everyone to come to repentance.

2 Peter 3:9 NIV

If we confess our sins, he is faithful and just and will
forgive us our sins and purify us from all unrighteousness.

1 John 1:9 NIV

Then you will experience God's peace, which exceeds anything we can understand.
His peace will guard your hearts and minds as you live in Christ Jesus.

Philippians 4:7 NLT

---

*Therefore, since we have been made right in God's sight by faith,
we have peace with God because of what Jesus Christ our Lord has done for us.*

Romans 5:1 NLT

CONTEMPLATE IN PRAYER

Dear Lord,

If I could have a do-over, I would apply it to my many past mistakes. I wouldn't have made that wrong turn, I wouldn't have lost my temper, I wouldn't have done the things I'm ashamed of, and I would have kept my promises.

Those things in my past are stuck there because I can't go back in time. But if I could go back, a lot of my current circumstances would be different.

Good news! You tell me that if I repent, my sins will be wiped out—erased! That's as good as a redo because it means You will not hold my past against me. It gives me such refreshing peace to know that You do not keep a list of my wrongs when I come to You in repentance.

I know You will forgive me, for You are the One who always keeps His promises, extending Your divine patience to me. You don't want anyone to perish, so You wait, hoping that all for whom Jesus died will repent.

And Your good news is famous, for You are faithful and just. You forgive sins and purify all who call on You from their unrighteousness.

Now that I know my faith, my belief in You, has made me right with You, I have peace with You—all because of what Jesus Christ our Lord has done for me.

I experience Your peace, which exceeds anything I can understand. Your peace guards my heart and mind as I live in Christ Jesus.

Thank You for wiping out my mistakes and giving me this opportunity to live for You.

In the name of Jesus, Amen.

REFLECT FROM YOUR HEART

1. Second Peter 3:9 mentions that God is patient with us, not wanting anyone to perish but for all to come to repentance. How have you experienced God's patience in your life? How does His patience lead you toward repentance and peace?

2. First John 1:9 assures us that if we confess our sins, God is faithful to forgive us and purify us. What role does confession play in your spiritual life, and how does it help you experience God's peace?

3. Philippians 4:7 speaks of the peace of God that transcends understanding, guarding our hearts and minds. How does God's peace protect you in your daily life, especially when you're dealing with regret or past mistakes?

–74–

MEDITATE ON THE WORD

They will fight you, but they will fail. For I am with you,
and I will take care of you. I, the Lord, have spoken!

Jeremiah 1:19 NLT

Consider it pure joy, my brothers and sisters,
whenever you face trials of many kinds,
because you know that the testing of your faith produces perseverance.

James 1:2-3 NIV

And after you have suffered a little while, the God of all grace,
who has called you to his eternal glory in Christ,
will himself restore, confirm, strengthen, and establish you.

1 Peter 5:10 ESV

No, despite all these things, overwhelming victory
is ours through Christ, who loved us.

Romans 8:37 NLT

I can do all this through him who gives me strength.

Philippians 4:13 NIV

CONTEMPLATE IN PRAYER

Dear Lord,

When I woke up this morning, the army of my enemy was at my door. I tried to slam it shut, but their leader told me I was surrounded with no escape. They threatened to destroy me.

That's when I turned to You, my Lord. You only laughed and told me, "They will fight against you, but they will fail. For I am with you, and I will take care of you."

Your words remind me of the time the prophet Elisha's servant saw that both he and his master were surrounded by the Aramean army. The poor servant panicked, but not Elisha. He simply prayed for his servant's eyes to be opened. That's when the servant saw the hills filled with an army of angels, horses, and chariots of fire. God struck the enemy's army with blindness, and then Elisha led them captive into the camp of his king.

In the same way, You, Lord, also surround my enemies and keep them at bay.

But the one thing I've noted about my trials is how they help me develop persevering faith. I've discovered Your joy as I begin to use my faith to see into the future. My battles will be victories in You.

Even if I suffer, You are the God of grace who will restore, confirm, strengthen, and establish me. I am finally beginning to understand that I really can do all You've called me to—through You, the One who gives me strength.

It turns out the enemy at my door cannot have victory over me when I am in You.

You give me peace as well as undeniable victory through Christ.

In the name of Jesus, Amen.

REFLECT FROM YOUR HEART

1. Jeremiah 1:19 promises that though enemies may fight against us, they will not prevail. What enemies or challenges do you feel are surrounding you today? How does the promise of God's presence and salvation give you resilience?

2. Elisha's servant's eyes were opened, and he saw God's protective army. Have there been times when you felt surrounded by difficulties but later realized God's protection was there all along? How does this story encourage you in your current battles?

3. The prayer mentions using faith to see future victories. How can having a vision beyond your current struggles help you endure and remain resilient? What are some practical ways to keep your focus on the victory God promises?

–75–

MEDITATE ON THE WORD

He lets me rest in green meadows;
he leads me beside peaceful streams.
PSALM 23:2 NLT

Truly my soul finds rest in God;
my salvation comes from him.
PSALM 62:1 NIV

In peace I will lie down and sleep,
for you alone, LORD, make me dwell in safety.
PSALM 4:8 NIV

When you lie down, you will not be afraid;
when you lie down, your sleep will be sweet.
PROVERBS 3:24 NIV

Come to me, all who labor and are heavy laden,
and I will give you rest.
MATTHEW 11:28 ESV

CONTEMPLATE IN PRAYER

Dear Lord,

I know nothing good will come to me unless I work hard and do it myself. But all this hard work is exhausting. It's like I'm trying to push a car with locked brakes up a mountain. The tires won't roll, and I can only manage an inch or so at a time because the car keeps sliding back toward me. Sweat pours down my brow, and I'm starting to wonder: *If I can't make progress, why am I even trying?*

Then I see You standing there, holding the key. You say, "Come to me, all who labor and are heavy laden, and I will give you rest." You unlock the car door and ask me, "Can I give you a lift?"

I'm dumbfounded. "You mean I don't have to strive? All I have to do is let You drive?"

You smile and motion for me to join You. I climb inside, and You take me to green pastures and lead me to peaceful streams.

We get out of the car and enjoy the day together. But it's Your presence that refreshes me. I find rest only in You, for You alone can save me from my striving.

When night comes, I know it will be sleepless. Who can rest with so many things to worry about? But You offer to hold my worries, giving me peace so I can rest. You make my night peaceful as I dwell in Your safety.

For now, when I lie down, I no longer need to be afraid. And my sleep will be sweet because I can trust You with my problems.

In the name of Jesus, Amen.

REFLECT FROM YOUR HEART

1. The prayer mentions the exhausting effort of pushing a car up a mountain, only to have it slide back. How does this metaphor reflect the struggles in your life? What does it mean to you to let God drive and provide the rest you need?

2. The prayer contrasts personal striving with relying on God's strength. In what areas of your life do you feel the need to let go and let God take control?

3. Psalm 4:8 and Proverbs 3:24 both speak of restful sleep in God's care. What practices or prayers do you engage in before bed to help you sleep in God's peace? How can you invite more of God's presence into your nightly routine?

–76–

Restrain My Tongue

MEDITATE ON THE WORD

The tongue also is a fire, a world of evil among the parts of the body.
It corrupts the whole body, sets the whole course
of one's life on fire, and is itself set on fire by hell.

James 3:6 NIV

Set a guard, O Lord, over my mouth;
keep watch over the door of my lips!

Psalm 141:3 ESV

Whoever guards his mouth preserves his life;
he who opens wide his lips comes to ruin.

Proverbs 13:3 ESV

Those who guard their mouths and
their tongues keep themselves from calamity.

Proverbs 21:23 NIV

Know this, my beloved brothers: let every person be quick to hear, slow to speak, slow to anger.

James 1:19 ESV

CONTEMPLATE IN PRAYER

Dear Lord,

When I don't get my tongue under control, it lights fires around me that consume even the people You've placed in my life. My words can even set my own hair on fire, which is not only unpleasant but unsightly (and a little painful).

The words I speak can produce such evil that they can fan the flames of hell and push people toward the edge.

Lord, You do not call me to introduce hell to anyone. You call me to introduce my friends and enemies to You so that one day, when we enter the gates of heaven, we can worship You together.

Lord, I need You to set a guard over my mouth and lock the door of my lips so my words don't destroy my life or the lives of others.

Sometimes I feel as though my mouth is loaded with daggers, sharp words set to attack others just so I can get my way. Show me how to remove or stop my evil speech until You transform these daggers into sweet words that honor You. That way, my words will no longer wound everyone around me.

Give me the wisdom to use my ears instead of my lips, so I will be quick to listen with Your understanding, love, and patience. For You speak to me of patience and peace, not impatience and anger. In this way, inspire me to use words of love instead of hate.

For learning how to guard my mouth can save my life, but speaking the wrong words at the wrong time could lead me to ruin.

In the name of Jesus, Amen.

REFLECT FROM YOUR HEART

1. James 3:6 describes the tongue as a fire capable of great destruction. How have you personally experienced the destructive power of words? What does it mean to surrender your speech to God's control?

2. How can surrendering your intentions to God keep you from using your words as daggers?

3. The prayer asks God to transform harmful speech into sweet words that honor Him. How can you invite God to transform your communication style? What does it mean to surrender the outcome of your conversations to God for your relationships?

–77–

Salvation

MEDITATE ON THE WORD

God loved the world this way: He gave his only Son so that everyone who believes in him will not die but will have eternal life.

JOHN 3:16 GW

Salvation is found in no one else, for there is no other name under heaven given to mankind by which we must be saved.

ACTS 4:12 NIV

If you openly declare that Jesus is Lord and believe in your heart that God raised him from the dead, you will be saved.

ROMANS 10:9 NLT

Everyone who calls on the name of the Lord will be saved.

ROMANS 10:13 NIV

For by grace you have been saved through faith. And this is not your own doing; it is the gift of God.

EPHESIANS 2:8 ESV

CONTEMPLATE IN PRAYER

Dear Lord,

I know You love me so much that You gave Your one and only Son to die in my place. But I must believe in Him as my risen Savior so that I will not perish but have everlasting life.

Lord, I must say, Your plan to defeat the enemy was brilliant. I know Satan never suspected that his master plan to crucify Jesus was the trap You would use to defeat his plans. What Satan didn't understand was that it would be impossible for Jesus to remain dead. He was not under the curse of sin because He'd led a sinless life. And because Jesus was both man and God, He rose from the dead, conquering both sin and death for all mankind, once and for all.

This is why salvation is found in no one else, for there is no other name under heaven given to mankind by which we can be saved.

Now that I see Christ's victory over Satan, I cannot unsee it. I would be a condemned fool unless I said yes to this gift that Jesus offered me.

So, I declare that Jesus is Lord and believe in my heart that You raised Him from the dead, and I am saved. For everyone who calls on the name of the Lord will be saved.

What a wonderful gift You have given to me. For by grace, I have been saved through faith. This was not of my own doing; it is the gift from You, my God.

Thank You, Lord, for this gift. Thank You, Jesus, for standing in my place.

In the name of Jesus, Amen.

REFLECT FROM YOUR HEART

1. Acts 4:12 emphasizes that salvation is found only in Jesus. How does this truth shape your approach to sharing your faith with others? How can you surrender any doubts or fears when proclaiming this message?

2. Romans 10:9 highlights the importance of openly declaring Jesus as Lord. What does it mean to declare Jesus as Lord in your daily life? How does surrendering your will to His lordship influence your actions and decisions?

3. Reflecting on Ephesians 2:8, how does faith play a role in your salvation journey? How does surrendering your doubts and trusting in God's promises deepen your faith?

–78–

Sorrow

MEDITATE ON THE WORD

Even though I walk through the darkest valley, I will fear no evil,
for you are with me; your rod and your staff, they comfort me.

Psalm 23:4 niv

He comforts us in all our troubles so that we can comfort others.
When they are troubled, we will be able to
give them the same comfort God has given us.

2 Corinthians 1:4 nlt

He will wipe every tear from their eyes, and there will be no
more death or sorrow or crying or pain. All these things are gone forever.

Revelation 21:4 nlt

He heals the brokenhearted and bandages their wounds.

Psalm 147:3 nlt

I have told you all this so that you may have peace in me.
Here on earth you will have many trials and sorrows.
But take heart, because I have overcome the world.

John 16:33 nlt

CONTEMPLATE IN PRAYER

Dear Lord,

You were a man of sorrows, burdened with the knowledge that Your wonderful earthly life—filled with love, ministry, and miracles—would end in the pain of the cross. Yet even in Your sorrow, You willingly laid down Your life for all who would believe in You. You are the Great Shepherd who walked through the darkest valley, and You did it for me.

When the time comes for me to face this dark valley myself, I know I will not walk through it alone. For You, my Jesus, are with me. I will fear no evil because You are ready to protect me with Your rod and Your staff. Your protection brings comfort during this difficult time in my journey.

You heal my broken heart and bandage my wounds.

You whisper through Your Word that You are with me, bringing me peace.

You lead me through my earthly trials and sorrows while holding my hand.

I can take heart, for You conquered sin and death, and You have overcome the world.

And in the sweetest of gestures, You allow me to take the comfort You've given me and use it to comfort others.

As I begin to climb out of the dark valley and back into the light, I can see the glow of heaven in the distance. I know that when I arrive at my final destination, You will be there to wipe every tear from my eyes. I will be with You in eternity, where there will be no more death, sorrow, crying, or pain. All these things will be gone forever.

In the name of Jesus, Amen.

REFLECT FROM YOUR HEART

1. Psalm 23:4 speaks of walking through the darkest valley without fear because of God's presence. How can recognizing His presence in your trials bring you peace?

2. Second Corinthians 1:4 talks about receiving God's comfort so that we can comfort others. How have you been able to use the comfort you've received from God to help others? How can surrendering to God's comfort empower you to be a source of support for those in need?

3. Revelation 21:4 tells of a time when sorrow and pain will be no more. How can holding onto the hope of this future help you navigate present sorrows with faith?

–79–

Spiritual Warfare

MEDITATE ON THE WORD

For our struggle is not against flesh and blood, but against the rulers, against the authorities, against the powers of this dark world and against the spiritual forces of evil in the heavenly realms.

EPHESIANS 6:12 NIV

The weapons we fight with are not the weapons of the world. On the contrary, they have divine power to demolish strongholds.

2 CORINTHIANS 10:4 NIV

So place yourselves under God's authority. Resist the devil, and he will run away from you.

JAMES 4:7 GW

Put on the full armor of God, so that you can take your stand against the devil's schemes.

EPHESIANS 6:11 NIV

But in that coming day no weapon turned against you will succeed. You will silence every voice raised up to accuse you. These benefits are enjoyed by the servants of the LORD; their vindication will come from me. I, the LORD, have spoken!

ISAIAH 54:17 NLT

CONTEMPLATE IN PRAYER

Dear Lord,

Once I was a slave, locked in a cell of hopelessness and destined for the gallows. But one day, Jesus, the great Prince, traded His life for mine. Alive from the dead, He came to my cell's door with the key to set me free so I could escape to a new life in Him.

My former captor, the old dragon, still hates me because Christ rescued me from his fiery grasp. But I've learned to be on guard against his attacks, for my struggle is not against flesh and blood, but against the rulers, authorities, and powers of this dark world, and against the spiritual forces of evil in the heavenly realms.

So, I place myself under Your authority, God. I resist the devil with the weapons You have given me. These weapons are not of this world but have divine power to demolish strongholds and to claim the victory that is already mine.

I put on Your full armor—the helmet of salvation, the breastplate of Your righteousness, the shield of faith, the shoes of peace, and the sword of the Spirit—and I stand firm against all the devil's schemes.

As I do, You silence every voice raised to accuse me. This is just one of the many benefits bestowed upon me through the gift of the cross of Jesus. His blessings bring me great joy and satisfaction as I celebrate in You.

Thank You for the authority You've given me to stand firm in Christ, resisting the enemy's lies. I will trust Your protection over my life daily, knowing victory is assured.

You, the Lord God, have spoken on my behalf, and I am saved!

In the name of Jesus, Amen.

REFLECT FROM YOUR HEART

1. How does the metaphor of being a slave in a cell, destined for the gallows, reflect our spiritual state before Christ? In what ways does this image help us understand the gravity of our spiritual situation?

2. The prayer describes Jesus as the great Prince who traded His life for ours. How does this image of Christ influence your understanding of His sacrifice? How can this perspective deepen your gratitude for salvation?

3. Despite the ongoing spiritual battle, the prayer emphasizes the peace that comes from God. How can we cultivate a sense of peace in the midst of spiritual warfare? How does this peace serve as a testimony to others?

–80–

Strength

MEDITATE ON THE WORD

But you, O Lord, do not be far off!
O you my help, come quickly to my aid!
Psalm 22:19 esv

It is God who arms me with strength and keeps my way secure.
Psalm 18:32 niv

God is our refuge and strength,
always ready to help in times of trouble.
Psalm 46:1 nlt

For I can do everything through Christ, who gives me strength.
Philippians 4:13 nlt

But those who trust in the Lord will find new strength.
They will soar high on wings like eagles.
They will run and not grow weary. They will walk and not faint.
Isaiah 40:31 nlt

CONTEMPLATE IN PRAYER

Dear Lord,

I face bullies in almost every area of my life—thieves who try to steal my joy, provision, and peace. Yet, there are times I feel too weak to stand and fight until I turn to see that You are standing with me. You teach me to call on You, and so I cry, "Lord, be near, be my help, come quickly to my aid!"

That's when the miracle begins. Just when the enemy plans to use me as a punching bag, You are there to protect me as I stand in You. You are my strength, always ready to help me in times of trouble.

I must admit, the look on the enemy's face when he sees me standing in Your strength is hilarious. He never expected You to show up. He thought I was too weak and discouraged to resist his assault, but he forgot You are with me.

You arm me with Your strength, and You keep the roads to my life secure.

I have learned that as I trust in You, Lord, You give me new strength. You catapult me to soar with the eagles, and You lengthen my steps as I race toward the finish line. You walk with me and make me strong.

Suddenly, I understand who I am. For I am in Christ, and through Christ, I can do anything, because Christ gives me strength.

Now, when the bullies see me coming, they run in the opposite direction because they know they will lose the fight, for I finally know who I am. I am Yours.

In the name of Jesus, Amen.

REFLECT FROM YOUR HEART

1. The prayer mentions facing bullies in various areas of life. How do these bullies manifest in your daily life (e.g., through negative thoughts, challenging situations, or difficult people)? How can recognizing these bullies help you call on God's strength?

2. The prayer describes the enemy's surprise when we stand in God's strength. How does this imagery encourage you in spiritual battles? What practical steps can you take to remind yourself to rely on God's strength rather than your own?

3. If it's true that in Christ you can do anything, how does your identity in Christ empower you to face life's challenges? What specific areas of your life need to be strengthened by this truth?

–81–

Surrender

MEDITATE ON THE WORD

Then Jesus said to his disciples, "If any of you wants to be my follower, you must give up your own way, take up your cross, and follow me."

Matthew 16:24 NLT

And so, dear brothers and sisters, I plead with you to give your bodies to God because of all he has done for you. Let them be a living and holy sacrifice—the kind he will find acceptable. This is truly the way to worship him.

Romans 12:1 NLT

I have been crucified with Christ and I no longer live, but Christ lives in me. The life I now live in the body, I live by faith in the Son of God, who loved me and gave himself for me.

Galatians 2:20 NIV

Humble yourselves, therefore, under the mighty hand of God so that at the proper time he may exalt you, casting all your anxieties on him, because he cares for you.

1 Peter 5:6-7 ESV

Trust in the Lord with all your heart; do not depend on your own understanding. Seek his will in all you do, and he will show you which path to take.

Proverbs 3:5-6 NLT

CONTEMPLATE IN PRAYER

Dear Lord,

The news floored me, turning my life upside down. I thought everything was fine, but now this? I can't figure out what to do.

Your still voice asks me, "Who said you must figure it out? Why not give it to Me and let Me figure it out for you?"

You would do that for me? But that means I would have to give You control of my life.

"You think you were in control?"

I did, until five minutes ago. But then Proverbs 3:5-6 came to mind: "Trust in the Lord with all your heart; do not depend on your own understanding. Seek his will in all you do, and he will show you which path to take." You mean You are really calling me to live a life of faith?

I feel Your peace and remember what Jesus said to His disciples: "If any of you wants to be my follower, you must give up your own way, take up your cross, and follow me."

Lord, I see the wisdom of giving up my own way. But You require even more; You ask me to give You not only my life but even my body, to live my life as an act of worship, as a holy sacrifice to You.

I say yes, for I have been crucified with Christ, and I no longer live, but Christ lives in me. The life I now live in the body, I live by faith in the Son of God, who loved me and gave Himself for me.

I give You my life and my circumstances and humble myself under Your mighty hand, casting my anxieties on You because You care for me.

In the name of Jesus, Amen.

REFLECT FROM YOUR HEART

1. Proverbs 3:5-6 speaks of trusting in the Lord and not depending on our own understanding. How does this perspective challenge the way we approach difficult situations in life?

2. The prayer includes a moment of realization that we are not in control of our lives. How do moments of crisis remind us to be more God-reliant?

3. The prayer reflects on the peace that comes with surrendering control to God. Can you think of a personal experience where surrendering to God brought you peace in the midst of a trial?

–82–

Temptation

MEDITATE ON THE WORD

Keep your mind clear, and be alert. Your opponent the devil is prowling around like a roaring lion as he looks for someone to devour.

1 Peter 5:8 GW

Submit yourselves, then, to God. Resist the devil, and he will flee from you.

James 4:7 NIV

Watch and pray so that you will not fall into temptation. The spirit is willing, but the flesh is weak.

Matthew 26:41 NIV

Lead us not into temptation, but deliver us from the evil one.

Matthew 6:13 NIV

No temptation has overtaken you except what is common to mankind. And God is faithful; he will not let you be tempted beyond what you can bear. But when you are tempted, he will also provide a way out so that you can endure it.

1 Corinthians 10:13 NIV

CONTEMPLATE IN PRAYER

Dear Lord,

One evening beneath the stars, my flashlight illuminated the paw prints of a mountain lion on the prowl.

I knew the creature was nearby, ready to spring at me from above. I dared not run lest the cat mistake me for its prey and pounce. Instead, I cleared my head of fear and stood tall, walking with deliberate steps. While I walked, alert to my surroundings, I belted out a song of praise as I scanned overhanging branches with my flashlight. There he was!

I yelled and threw rocks at him until the cat slinked away, more afraid of me than I was of him. I know that when I'm on watch, that old mountain lion will not have the opportunity to make me his next meal.

This mountain lion reminds me of the devil, prowling around and ready to devour me if I fail to stay vigilant. Because of this threat, I will submit myself to God and resist the devil, and he will flee from me.

I will watch and pray that I do not fall into temptation because I know my spirit is willing, but my flesh is weak.

When I pray, I will pray as Jesus taught: a prayer that God would not lead me into temptation but deliver me from the evil one.

If I avoid the temptations common to man, my path will be safe. I also know my faithful God will not let me be tempted beyond what I can bear. But when I am tempted, God will provide a way out so that I can endure it.

In the name of Jesus, Amen.

REFLECT FROM YOUR HEART

1. How does the imagery of a mountain lion on the prowl help you understand the nature of temptation? In what ways can being clearheaded and alert help you avoid falling into temptation?

2. The prayer mentions submitting to God as a way to resist the devil. What does submitting to God look like in your daily life? How does this submission empower you to resist temptation?

3. Although the focus is on resisting temptation, the prayer also speaks to the peace that comes from knowing God provides a way out. How does trusting God's guidance bring peace to your heart in the face of temptation?

–83–

Thankfulness

MEDITATE ON THE WORD

Give thanks to the LORD,
for he is good; his love endures forever.
1 CHRONICLES 16:34 NIV

I will give thanks to you, LORD, with all my heart;
I will tell of all your wonderful deeds.
PSALM 9:1 NIV

Let us come before him with thanksgiving
and extol him with music and song.
PSALM 95:2 NIV

The LORD is my strength and my shield; my heart trusts in him,
and he helps me. My heart leaps for joy,
and with my song I praise him.
PSALM 28:7 NIV

Give thanks in all circumstances;
for this is God's will for you in Christ Jesus.
1 THESSALONIANS 5:18 NIV

CONTEMPLATE IN PRAYER

Dear Lord,

One of the things I love about Christmas is presents. So I search beneath my tree to see who is giving thanks to me. *Oh dear, those words felt so wrong.*

Lord, please forgive me when I miss the chance to give thanks to You—the holy One, the creator, the majestic God of the universe. You are the one I worship, not me, nor the gifts You give me, but You.

I stop in this moment and thank You with my whole heart, for You are good; Your love endures forever. I will give thanks to You, Lord, and will tell of all Your wonderful deeds, for You have saved my life more times than I can count. You give me Your grace and goodness. You make a way for me where there is no other way. You provide for me and save me from danger. You hold my hand when I am afraid.

So, I come before You with thanksgiving and extol You with music and sing the words of the hymnist Reginald Heber, who wrote, "Holy, holy, holy! Lord God Almighty! All thy works shall praise thy name, in earth and sky and sea; Holy, holy, holy! merciful and mighty! God in three Persons, blessed Trinity!"

I will worship You even more, for You are my strength and my shield; my heart trusts in You, and You help me. My heart leaps for joy, and with my song, I praise You.

Even in my difficulties, I will give thanks in all my circumstances, for this is Your will for me in Christ Jesus. Thank You.

In the name of Jesus, Amen.

REFLECT FROM YOUR HEART

1. The prayer mentions using music and song to extol God. How does music influence your worship and thankfulness? Can you share a song that helps you express gratitude to God?

2. The prayer contrasts the self-centeredness of seeking thanks from others with the call to worship God. How can you shift your focus from seeking recognition for yourself to giving glory to God? What challenges might arise when making this shift?

3. The prayer ends with a commitment to give thanks in all circumstances. How can you make thankfulness a daily practice? What are some specific things you can thank God for today, even if they seem small or insignificant?

–84–

Time Pressure

MEDITATE ON THE WORD

There is a time for everything,
and a season for every activity under the heavens.

Ecclesiastes 3:1 niv

Be patient, then, brothers and sisters, until the Lord's coming.
See how the farmer waits for the land to yield its valuable crop,
patiently waiting for the autumn and spring rains.

James 5:7 niv

Wait for the Lord; be strong and take heart and wait for the Lord.

Psalm 27:14 niv

Be still before the Lord and wait patiently for him; do not fret when people succeed in their ways, when they carry out their wicked schemes.

Psalm 37:7 niv

I waited patiently for the Lord; he turned to me and heard my cry.

Psalm 40:1 niv

CONTEMPLATE IN PRAYER

Dear Lord,

Why does it seem that the theme of my life is "Hurry up and wait"?

I rush to get ready, dash my car out of my driveway, then push the limit all the way to the freeway, only to face a dead stop traffic jam. Despite my prayers, my car creeps along at a whopping five miles per hour all the way to my destination.

But I know that You have a different vantage on time because You explain there is a time for everything and a season for every activity under the heavens.

This idea is hard to understand. But I'm curious if You sometimes use my delays to cause me to miss a collision with a semi-truck. I guess I'll never know because it's hard to factor in the secrets of Your protection plan. But that makes me wonder if some of my delays are part of Your perfect timing for reasons I've never considered.

You call on me to be patient whenever I wait. Even the farmer has to wait for the rains before his crop is ready to harvest. So, like the farmer, I set myself to wait with You and for You. As I wait, You help me be strong and take heart.

David sang the virtues of being still before You and waited patiently for You.

Perhaps it's in the waiting where You mold me to be more like You. In that case, I will wait patiently for You, Lord, because You are with me always, and You are always teaching me peace and contentment.

(Perhaps if I could hurry up and learn this lesson sooner than later, I wouldn't have to wait so much.)

In the name of Jesus, Amen

REFLECT FROM YOUR HEART

1. The prayer mentions the secrets of God's protection plan. How does trusting in God's unseen protection help you manage your frustrations with time pressure? Can you share an experience where you realized God was protecting or guiding you through a delay?

2. Psalm 27:14 encourages us to be strong while waiting for the Lord. What does it mean to wait with strength? How can you find strength and encouragement during seasons of waiting?

3. The prayer humorously suggests that learning patience sooner might reduce waiting. How does surrendering control over time and outcomes to God help you experience more peace? What steps can you take to practice surrender in your daily life?

–85–

Transformation

MEDITATE ON THE WORD

He saved us, not because of the righteous things we had done,
but because of his mercy. He washed away our sins,
giving us a new birth and new life through the Holy Spirit.

Titus 3:5 NLT

And I will give you a new heart, and I will put a new spirit in you.
I will take out your stony, stubborn heart and give you a tender, responsive heart.

Ezekiel 36:26 NLT

For we are God's masterpiece. He has created us anew in Christ Jesus,
so we can do the good things he planned for us long ago.

Ephesians 2:10 NLT

And we all, who with unveiled faces contemplate the Lord's glory,
are being transformed into his image with ever-increasing glory,
which comes from the Lord, who is the Spirit.

2 Corinthians 3:18 NIV

Therefore, if anyone is in Christ, the new creation has come:
The old has gone, the new is here!

2 Corinthians 5:17 NIV

CONTEMPLATE IN PRAYER

Dear Lord,

I once heard a story about a kind barber who invited a homeless man into his shop for a shower, shave, and haircut. When the man was scrubbed and smelling of soap, he sat down in the barber's chair, wearing clean clothes for the first time in years. That's when the barber went to work, plucking the man's unkempt brows, shaving away his tangled beard, and shampooing, then conditioning his matted hair before trimming and combing it into a flattering style.

When the barber was finished, he turned the man to face the mirror. The gentleman was shocked. He looked like a brand-new person, at least on the outside.

But the inside of my heart can be as tangled and neglected as a messy beard.

Jesus saved us, not because of our grooming or the righteous things we've done, but because of His mercy. He washed away our sins and gave us a new birth and new life through the Holy Spirit. He took away our stony, stubborn heart and gave us a tender, responsive heart, along with a new spirit.

When we become new in Christ, it's like a heart-and-soul makeover. The new creation has come: The old is gone, the new is here! When we step out into our new life, it's clear to everyone that we are God's masterpiece. He has created us anew in Christ Jesus so we can do the good things He planned for us long ago.

And all of us, who with unveiled faces contemplate the Lord's glory, are being transformed into His image with ever-increasing glory, which comes from the Lord, who is the Spirit.

In the name of Jesus, Amen.

REFLECT FROM YOUR HEART

1. The prayer mentions a story of external transformation through a makeover. How does this compare to the internal transformation that Christ offers? In what ways is spiritual transformation deeper and more significant than external changes?

2. Titus 3:5 emphasizes that our transformation is due to God's mercy, not our righteousness. How does this understanding impact your view of grace and your relationship with God? How can recognizing God's mercy lead to deeper peace?

3. Ezekiel 36:26 speaks of God giving us a new heart and spirit. What does it mean to have a tender, responsive heart? How have you experienced this change in your life, and how does it affect your interactions with others or give you peace?

–86–

Troubles

MEDITATE ON THE WORD

The Lord is a refuge for the oppressed,
a stronghold in times of trouble.
Psalm 9:9 niv

The righteous cry out, and the Lord hears them;
he delivers them from all their troubles.
Psalm 34:17 niv

Though I walk in the midst of trouble, you preserve my life;
you stretch out your hand against the wrath of my enemies,
and your right hand delivers me.
Psalm 138:7 esv

When you pass through the waters, I will be with you; and when you pass through the rivers, they will not sweep over you. When you walk through the fire, you will not be burned; the flames will not set you ablaze.
Isaiah 43:2 niv

In this world you will have trouble.
But take heart! I have overcome the world.
John 16:33 niv

CONTEMPLATE IN PRAYER

Dear Lord,

I wish I could hide from my troubles, but they walk into my life, making a mess of everything. It's like we're sharing a prison cell with no chance of escape. Then I remember what David said when he was running from trouble: "The LORD is a refuge for the oppressed, a stronghold in times of trouble."

David knew You would deliver him. And if You would deliver him, would also deliver me. So, I cry, "Lord, I need You! Please be my refuge!"

Then it hits me, Lord, You are my refuge—right now. Though I walk straight into a pit of vipers, You protect me. You stretch out Your right hand against the venom of my foes.

Isaiah the prophet quoted You: "When you pass through the waters, I will be with you; and when you pass through the rivers, they will not sweep over you. When you walk through the fire, you will not be burned; the flames will not set you ablaze."

There is nowhere I can go where the enemy can keep You from me. So, when troubles press in, You invite me to hide in You. When the waters rise, You are my life preserver. When I pass through the rivers, You keep me afloat. When I walk through the fire, You keep me cool. It's just as Jesus said, "In this world, you will have trouble. But take heart! I have overcome the world."

This means I have overcome the world in You.

Because You are with me in all circumstances, I will not fear the trouble that comes my way. You provide strength and peace, and in You, I find victory.

In the name of Jesus, Amen.

REFLECT FROM YOUR HEART

1. Psalm 34:17 says, "The righteous cry out, and the LORD hears them." What does it mean to cry out to God in your troubles? How can expressing your struggles to God bring you closer to Him? Stop and tell God your troubles right now.

2. Reflecting on Psalm 138:7, how have you seen God preserve your life or save you from your foes? What does it mean to you that God actively stretches out His hand to protect you?

3. The prayer mentions the idea of hiding in God. What does it mean to hide in God during times of trouble? How can this concept provide comfort, peace, and strength in your daily life?

–87–

Trust

MEDITATE ON THE WORD

Trust in him at all times, you people;
pour out your hearts to him, for God is our refuge.
PSALM 62:8 NIV

But I trust in you, LORD; I say, "You are my God."
PSALM 31:14 NIV

Commit your way to the LORD;
trust in him, and he will act.
PSALM 37:5 ESV

The LORD is good, a refuge in times of trouble.
He cares for those who trust in him.
NAHUM 1:7 NIV

***

Blessed is the one who trusts in the LORD,
whose confidence is in him.
JEREMIAH 17:7 NIV

***

CONTEMPLATE IN PRAYER

Dear Lord,

Remember? I used to know how to escape my ball and chain of worry. When I'd experience a beautiful day, I'd kick off my bonds and take a walk with You and experience Your glorious freedom. But now, with so much weighing me down, I haven't been able to spend much time with You.

As I sit here on my couch, I turn my Bible to Psalm 62:8: "Trust in him at all times, you people; pour out your hearts to him, for God is our refuge," (NIV).

That's beautiful. As I read that, I felt some of the weight I've been dragging lift off my shoulders. Next, I flip to Psalm 31:14: "But I trust in you, LORD; I say, 'You are my God.'"

Now I'm wondering why I've been stuck in my worries. It's like I've forgotten that if I commit my ways to You and trust You with my problems, You will act on my behalf.

Maybe I've been working on my self-confidence instead of working on trusting in You.

Just realizing this truth broke a few of my chains, and I'm suddenly able to stand. Lord, I think maybe I should give You all my worries. Isn't this what You're asking of me? You want me to let go and let You move on my behalf without my help.

Wow! I get it! And now I'm free. Suddenly, I can walk wherever You want to take me because I trust that You are good. From now on, I'll hide my troubles in You because You care about me, and You will turn my troubles into blessings.

In the name of Jesus, Amen.

REFLECT FROM YOUR HEART

1. The prayer mentions being weighed down by worries. How does trusting God help you break free from the ball and chain of worry? How can you practice releasing your worries to God daily through prayer and faith?

2. The prayer discusses the freedom of letting go and allowing God to act without personal interference. How does surrendering control to God's will change your perspective on your problems and worries, especially during difficult situations?

3. Nahum 1:7 reminds us that God is good and a refuge in times of trouble. How does trusting in God's goodness provide peace, strength, and reassurance during life's storms and challenges?

–88–

Wisdom

MEDITATE ON THE WORD

The fear of the LORD is the beginning of wisdom,
and knowledge of the Holy One is understanding.
PROVERBS 9:10 NIV

For the LORD gives wisdom; from his mouth
come knowledge and understanding.
PROVERBS 2:6 ESV

Getting wisdom is the wisest thing you can do!
And whatever else you do, develop good judgment.
PROVERBS 4:7 NLT

Those who trust their own insight are foolish,
but anyone who walks in wisdom is safe.
PROVERBS 28:26 NLT

---

*If any of you lacks wisdom, you should ask God,
who gives generously to all without finding fault,
and it will be given to you.*
JAMES 1:5 NIV

CONTEMPLATE IN PRAYER

Dear Lord,

A blind man cannot fear a cliff if he has no understanding of its dangers, that is, until he walks off the edge and experiences a fall.

In the same way, a spiritually blind man cannot fear You if he doesn't see You, that is, until he walks off the edge of his life to meet You on his day of judgment.

But the one who knows You understands to fear You, for You are the great God. You are the all-powerful One, the One who can both create life and take it away. To fear You is the beginning of wisdom, and knowing the Holy One brings understanding.

But knowing You is the greatest blessing. For the man who knows You receives wisdom, and wisdom helps him find knowledge and understanding to build a better life, strengthening his faith and guiding him in righteousness. The one who is wise and develops good judgment, which helps him avoid pitfalls and prevents him from falling over cliffs.

When I need wisdom, I will ask You, and You will give me all the wisdom I need, for You are generous to me and never find fault with me for seeking You.

But the wisest thing I could ever do is to trust in Your wisdom and not lean into my own foolish insights. For when I listen to Your Word and wise counsel, I walk in safety because I trust You in all things. Instead of stumbling or walking off cliffs, I will walk across the mountaintops. I will live a life of victory through the power of the Spirit.

In the name of Jesus, Amen.

REFLECT FROM YOUR HEART

1. Proverbs 9:10 states, "The fear of the LORD is the beginning of wisdom," (NIV). How do you interpret the concept of fearing the Lord for your own life, and how does it contribute to gaining wisdom?

2. The prayer mentions that wisdom helps a person avoid pitfalls and dangerous cliffs in life. Can you think of a cliff in your life that you've avoided because of God's wisdom? How did His guidance help you navigate that situation?

3. The prayer concludes with the idea that walking in wisdom leads to conquering mountains and living a victorious life. What mountains in your life are you facing right now, and how can wisdom help you conquer them?

–89–

Worry

MEDITATE ON THE WORD

The LORD is my light and my salvation—whom shall I fear?
The LORD is the stronghold of my life—of whom shall I be afraid?

PSALM 27:1 NIV

Do not worry about your life, what you will eat or drink; or about your body, what you will wear. Is not life more than food, and the body more than clothes?

MATTHEW 6:25 NIV

And if God cares so wonderfully for wildflowers that are here today and thrown into the fire tomorrow, he will certainly care for you. Why do you have so little faith?

MATTHEW 6:30 NLT

Can any one of you by worrying add a single hour to your life?

MATTHEW 6:27 NIV

Do not worry about tomorrow, for tomorrow will worry about itself.
Each day has enough trouble of its own.

MATTHEW 6:34 NIV

CONTEMPLATE IN PRAYER

Dear Lord,

It's past midnight, and my motorboat bounces across the wavetops as rain pelts my face. I've lost all sense of direction as I search the dark horizons. I'm afraid I'm headed out to sea when I'm desperate to find a safe port. And I'm also afraid I'll smash my boat into the reef and sink beneath the blackness.

Then I see it—a tiny pulsating light on the horizon. It's the lighthouse! I feel such relief knowing I will soon sip steaming tea in a warm harbor, safe from the storm.

You, Lord, are my lighthouse and my salvation—whom shall I fear? You are my safe place—of whom shall I be afraid?

When You are with me, I do not need to worry about my life, not even what I will eat or drink. I will be free of worrying about what I will wear. For my life is about more than food or clothes, it's about trusting You for all my needs.

If nothing else, I know You will take care of me. When I finally believe this, I have the faith to trust in You.

Besides, if my worries can't add a single hour to my life, why am I wasting hours of my time lost in worry and fear? There is no good reason for me to fritter away my life tormented by negative possibilities when I know You will take care of me.

So, I've made a choice: I will not worry about tomorrow, for tomorrow will worry about itself. Each day has enough trouble of its own. I decide to believe that You are with me, and I am blessed.

In the name of Jesus, Amen.

REFLECT FROM YOUR HEART

1. The prayer uses the metaphor of a stormy sea and a lighthouse to describe the experience of worry and finding safety in God. How do you personally navigate stormy periods in your life, and how does God act as your guiding lighthouse in these times?

2. Matthew 6:34 encourages us to focus on today rather than worrying about tomorrow. How can you practice staying present and trusting God with your future, even in difficult circumstances?

3. The prayer talks about the waste of time spent on negative possibilities. How can you train your mind to focus on more peaceful, positive, faith-filled thoughts instead of being consumed by worry?

–90–

Worship

MEDITATE ON THE WORD

Let us come to him with thanksgiving.
Let us sing psalms of praise to him.
Psalm 95:2 NLT

Worship the Lord with gladness;
come before him with joyful songs.
Psalm 100:2 NIV

Come, let us bow down in worship,
let us kneel before the Lord our Maker.
Psalm 95:6 NIV

For great is the Lord and most worthy of praise;
he is to be feared above all gods.
Psalm 96:4 NIV

---

*Ascribe to the Lord the glory due his name;
worship the Lord in the splendor of his holiness.*
Psalm 29:2 NIV

CONTEMPLATE IN PRAYER

Dear Lord,

I want to stop and thank You for this time we've spent together. I've felt Your presence, I've given You my worries and fears, and I've learned how to trust You instead of letting my anxieties torment me. So now, I come to You with a thankful heart, with a song of praise on my lips.

My worship is meant for You alone, yet I notice that as I worship, You help me release my cares and come to You with gladness and joyful songs. Worshiping You helps me put things into proper perspective—You, the Great God, and me, the one who bows before You.

I love to humble myself, to put my "give me" prayers away, and to kneel before my Lord and Maker with love and adoration.

My praise helps me fear You, for fearing You is how I show reverence. Because You forgive me, I do not need to cower, but I do need to lay my life before You as my way of showing love, honor, and respect.

For great are You and most worthy of praise; You are to be feared above all gods. Glory is due Your name because of Your greatness, and the enemy can never defeat You.

I will worship You, my Lord, in the splendor of Your holiness. I thank You for all You've done—setting me free from sin and death, making me Yours, and giving me peace and joy. I praise You for sending Jesus to die for my sins, for Your holiness and majesty, for Your enduring love, and for all You are and will be forevermore.

In the name of Jesus, Amen.

REFLECT FROM YOUR HEART

1. The prayer speaks of laying down "give me" prayers and kneeling in love and adoration. How can worship serve as a means to surrender your will and desires to God's plan?

2. The prayer emphasizes that worship helps to place God in His proper perspective. How does focusing on God's greatness during worship shift the way you view your life and its problems?

3. As you reflect on the prayer, how has worship helped you find freedom from worries and fears? How does it contribute to your sense of peace? What practices help you maintain a heart of worship? Take a moment to worship God now, thanking Him for this journey of praying His word to Him.